Elisabeth Prescher

ADJETIVOS E ADVÉRBIOS em INGLÊS

Adjectives and Adverbs

© 2013 Elisabeth Prescher

Preparação de texto
Gabriela Morandini / Verba Editorial

Capa e projeto gráfico
Paula Astiz

Editoração eletrônica
Laura Lotufo / Paula Astiz Design

Assistente editorial
Aline Naomi Sassaki

Dados Internacionais de Catalogação na Publicação (CIP)
(Câmara Brasileira do Livro, SP, Brasil)

Prescher, Elisabeth
   Adjetivos e advérbios em inglês : adjectives and adverbs / Elisabeth Prescher. — Barueri, SP : DISAL, 2013.

   ISBN 978-85-7844-152-4

   1. Adjetivos - Inglês - Estudo e ensino 2. Advérbios - Inglês - Estudo e ensino 3. Inglês - Gramática I. Título.

13-10020   CDD-425

Índices para catálogo sistemático:
1. Adjetivos : Inglês : Linguística   425
2. Advérbios : Inglês : Linguística   425

Todos os direitos reservados em nome de:
Bantim, Canato e Guazzelli Editora Ltda.

Alameda Mamoré 911 – cj. 107
Alphaville – BARUERI – SP
CEP: 06454-040
Tel./Fax: (11) 4195-2811
Visite nosso site: www.disaleditora.com.br
Televendas: (11) 3226-3111

Fax gratuito: 0800 7707 105/106
E-mail para pedidos: comercial@disal.com.br

Nenhuma parte desta publicação pode ser reproduzida, arquivada ou transmitida de nenhuma forma ou meio sem permissão expressa e por escrito da Editora.

Sumário

Adjectives

Kinds	7
Position	8
Linking verbs	9
Postpositive adjectives	9
Multiple functions	10
Practice	10

Demonstrative, Distributive and Possessive Adjectives

Demonstrative	15
Distributive	17
Possessive	18
Practice	20

Interrogative, Quantitative and Descriptive Adjectives

Interrogative	25
Quantitative	26
Descriptive	29
Practice	30

Order of Adjectives

Master Chart	35
Punctuation	36
Practice	37

Form of Adjectives

Present and Past Participle	43
Affixes	44
Compound Adjectives	46
Practice	48

Adverbs

Kinds	54
Linking Verbs	55
Multiple Functions	56
Practice	58

Position and Order of Adverbs

Position	63
Order	65
Master Chart	66
Practice	67

Form of Adverbs

Using -ly	73
Spelling	75
Multiple forms	75
Practice	77

Adjective or Adverb?

Adjective	83
Adverb	83
Linking Verbs	85
Practice	86

Comparison of Adjectives and Adverbs

Form	**90**
Spelling	**91**
Irregular Comparison	**92**
Constructions with Comparisons	**93**
Practice	**95**

Common Mistakes

Only, enough, too, very, fairly, rather, good, well, bad, badly, sure, surely, real, really, near, nearly, short, shortly, slow, slowly, barely, scarcely, hardly, already, still, yet	**101**
Inversion	**112**
Listing	**113**
Practice	**113**

Appendix

Most Common Adjectives	**117**
Most Common Adverbs	**124**
Adjectives and Prepositions	**127**
Answers	**129**

Adjectives

Happy people enjoy life.
We are **happy**.

BASICS

Adjetivos são palavras como *happy*, *square*, *sweet*, *short* etc.

Descrevem, quantificam, identificam substantivos ou pronomes. Têm uma forma única[1] usada tanto para o singular e plural quanto para o masculino e feminino.

a kind woman
a kind man
clever ladies
clever kids

KINDS OF ADJECTIVES (TIPOS DE ADJETIVOS)

(ver Most Common Adjectives na pág. 117)

Os adjetivos podem ser:

descriptive/quality (descritivos/de qualidade):
round, thin, blue, good, tall, tired etc.
(redondo, fino, azul, bom, alto, cansado)

quantitative (quantitativos):
two, first, enough, some, many, much etc.
(dois, primeiro, suficiente, algum, muitos, muito)

---

1. Exceção: os demonstrativos **this** e **these**, **that** e **those**.

possessive (possessivos):
my, your, his, her, our, their etc.
(meu, teu, dele, dela, nosso, deles)

interrogative (interrogativos):
what, which, whose
(que, qual, de quem)

demonstrative (demonstrativos):
this, that, these, those, first, such etc.
(este, aquele, estes, aqueles, primeiro, tal)

distributive (distributivos):
each, every, either, neither
(cada, cada, ambos, nenhum)

POSITION (POSIÇÃO)

∗ Adjetivos usualmente vêm antes de substantivos.

*He bought a **red** car.*
(Ele comprou um carro vermelho.)
*I went to an **incredible** show.*
(Fui a um show incrível.)
*We bought **two** dresses.*
(Compramos dois vestidos.)
*She has **many** friends.*
(Ela tem muitos amigos.)
*I shouted at the **barking** dog.*
(Gritei com o cão que latia.)

∗ **Linking Verbs[2]**

Adjetivos também podem vir após verbos de ligação (Linking Verbs).

be:	*She is **famous**.*	(Ela é famosa.)
become:	*He became **rich**.*	(Ele ficou rico.)
feel:	*I feel **good**.*	(Sinto-me bem.)
get:	*They got **tired**.*	(Eles ficaram cansados.)
grow:	*We are growing **old**.*	(Estamos ficando velhos.)
keep:	*Keep **quiet**, please.*	(Fique quieto, por favor.)
make:	*You make me **happy**.*	(Você me faz feliz.)
look:	*He looks **tired**.*	(Ele parece cansado.)
seem:	*You seem **upset**.*	(Você parece aborrecido.)
smell:	*The cake smells **good**.*	(O bolo cheira bem.)
taste:	*The fish tastes **awful**.*	(O peixe tem gosto horrível.)
turn:	*She turned **pale**.*	(Ela ficou pálida.)

COMPLEMENTARY

✳ Postpositive adjectives

Adjetivos podem vir após o substantivo em alguns tipos de construção (Postpositive Adjectives).

*He likes his coffee **hot**.*
(Ele gosta de seu café quente.)
*They consider the pyramids **interesting**.*
(Eles acham as pirâmides interessantes.)
*There was a cat **hidden** in the bush.*
(Havia um gato escondido no mato.)
*Tell me something **new**.*
(Conte-me algo novo.)
*The president **elect** lives in New York.*
(O presidente eleito mora em Nova York.)

---

2. Linking verbs: be, become, get, keep, make, appear, seem, look, smell, sound, taste, feel, grow, remain, prove, stay, and turn.

MULTIPLE FUNCTIONS (MÚLTIPLAS FUNÇÕES)

Certas palavras, dependendo da posição na frase, podem desempenhar diferentes funções.

adjetivo / advérbio: *fast, late, early, weekly etc.*
adjetivo / substantivo: *black, classic, poor, noble etc.*
adjetivo / pronome: *much, many, this, that, some etc.*
adjetivo / particípio: *lost, escaped, alarming, frightening*

adjective	**other**
*It is a **fast** car.*	*That car runs **fast**. (adv.)*
(É um carro rápido.)	(Aquele carro anda rápido.)
*The Clintons are **rich**.*	*They should help the **poor**. (noun)*
(Os Clintons são ricos.)	(Eles deveriam ajudar os pobres.)
***Many** kids like soccer.*	***Many** like baseball. (pron.)*
(Muitos garotos gostam de futebol.)	(Muitos gostam de beisebol.)
*That is a **frightening** place.*	*You are **frightening** me. (partic.)*
(Esse lugar é assustador.)	(Você está me assustando.)

PRACTICE

(respostas na pág. 129)

1. Underline the adjectives in the movie titles. Some titles have no adjective (Do not underline *a*, *an*, *the*).

1. *Little Black Swan*
2. *Five Easy Pieces*
3. *Creature from the Black Lagoon*
4. *The Brown Bunny*
5. *The Talented Mr. Ripley*
6. *Unfortunate Events*

7. *A Better World*
8. *A Book of Common Prayer*
9. *A Brand New Me*
10. *A Cold Case*
11. *A Burning Hot Summer*
12. *A Cat in Paris*
13. *A Dirty Job*
14. *A Dark Truth*
15. *The Sixth Man*
16. *12 Angry Men*
17. *American Beauty*
18. *American History X*
19. *At First Sight*
20. *A Beautiful Mind*
21. *Deep Impact*
22. *Defending Your Life*
23. *Super Mario Bros*
24. *Demetrius and the Gladiators*
25. *The Fellowship of the Ring*
26. *A Few Good Men*
27. *Fiddler on the Roof*
28. *Field of Dreams*
29. *The Fifth Element*
30. *Indiana Jones and the Last Crusade*

2. Choose the correct adjective.

1. *The wind became*
   a. stronger   *b. angry*

2. *The grapes tasted*
   a. sweet   *b. red*

3. *The leaves turned*
   a. brown   *b. late*

4. The children seem
    a. new   *b.* happy

5. The weather is growing
    a. hot   *b.* interesting

6. The story sounds
    a. square   *b.* false

7. The cake smelled
    a. cold   *b.* good

8. The pillow feels soft and
    a. real   *b.* comfortable

9. The car looks
    a. old   *b.* angry

10. I find the exercise
    a. easy   *b.* square

11. She made me
    a. empty   *b.* depressed

12. The answer is
    a. puzzling   *b.* tall

3. Use adjectives from the box to expand the sentences.

> depressed   mysterious   orange   big   calm   dusty   good
> mountainous   star-shaped   many   thick   white   heavy

1. A young woman with a <u>mysterious</u> past gets to the village.
2. The weather will be very cool and dry. Take a _____ coat.

3. *No one wants to be sad and _____ .*
4. *The leaves are red, yellow and _____ .*
5. *That is a _____ box. Let me help you.*
6. *Friends help you to feel _____ about yourself.*
7. *_____ fans turned out for the _____ game.*
8. *The old vase set on the _____ shelf.*
9. *Our restless guide led us up the _____ path.*
10. *We saw the _____ kite gliding through the air.*
11. *He covered his bedroom walls with _____ paint.*
12. *The racing boat dashed over the _____ surface of the lake.*

4. **Read the quotes. Classify the underlined words as A** (adjective) **or N** (noun).

1. *You don't make the **poor richer** by making the rich poorer.*
   Winston Churchill

   _____ *N, A* _____

2. *If a **free** society cannot help the many who are **poor**, it cannot save the few who are rich.*
   John F. Kennedy

   _____

3. *Do not waste your time on **Social** Questions. What is the matter with the **poor** is Poverty; what is the matter with the rich is Uselessness.*
   George Bernard Shaw

   _____

4. ***Charity** appeases our **consciences**.*
   Muhammad Yunus

   _____

5. *It's what you do in your **free** time that will set you **free** or enslave you.*
   Jarod Kintz

   _____

6. *Our people are good people; our people are kind people. Pray God some day kind people won't all be poor.*

John Steinbeck

———————

7. *I was so thin I could slice bread with my shoulder blades, only I seldom had bread.*

Charles Bukowski

———————

8. *Religion is what keeps the poor from murdering the rich.*

Napoleon Bonaparte

———————

9. *You have to be objective about money to use it fairly.*

Keith Haring

———————

10. *It's easy to be humble when your life's prosper.*

Toba Beta

———————

5. Check the sentences containing postpositive adjectives.

1. *The soccer players went to the best hotel available.* ☐
2. *He wants to do something useful.* ☐
3. *The poor lady missed the last train.* ☐
4. *What band was playing that terrible music?* ☐
5. *I like the steak well done.* ☐
6. *She addressed to everyone present.* ☐
7. *We have to take the shortest way possible.* ☐
8. *That was an interesting idea, wasn't it?* ☐
9. *They faced the worst conditions imaginable.* ☐
10. *She wants to marry somebody rich.* ☐

Demonstrative, Distributive and Possessive Adjectives

He lives in **that** house.
Each boy has **his** kite.

BASICS

DEMONSTRATIVE ADJECTIVES (ADJETIVOS DEMONSTRATIVOS)

Demonstrativos são palavras como *this*, *these*, *that*, *those*. *This* e *that* acompanham substantivos no singular. *These* e *those* acompanham substantivos no plural. Indicam qual é o objeto da fala. Podem funcionar como adjetivos ou pronomes.

This house is mine. (adj.)
(Esta casa é minha.)

This is good. (pron.)
(Este é bom.)

singular	*this* (este/a, isto)	*that* (aquele/a, aquilo, esse/a, isso)
plural	*these* (estes/as)	*those* (aqueles/as, esses/as)

* *This* e *these* indicam proximidade do emissor e podem se referir ao período em andamento.

***These** houses are for sale.*

(Estas casas estão à venda.)

*I must talk to him **this** month.*

(Preciso falar com ele este mês.)

***This** film is very funny!*

(Este filme é muito engraçado! = ainda acontecendo)

✳ ***That** e **those** indicam que coisas ou pessoas estão distantes do emissor e podem se referir a um período passado.*

***That** man looks sad.*

(Aquele homem parece triste.)

*There was no pollution in **that** time.*

(Não havia poluição naquele tempo.)

***That** game was bad.*

(Esse jogo foi péssimo. = o jogo acabou)

✳ Outras palavras podem funcionar como adjetivos demonstrativos.

such/a (tal, tais)

the former ... the latter (o primeiro ... o último)

*I had never read **such a** book.*

(Nunca tinha lido tal livro.)

*I would never buy **such** books.*

(Nunca compraria tais livros.)

*I prefer **the former** version of the story.*

(Prefiro a primeira versão da história)

*We didn't see **the latter** part of the film.*

(Não vimos a última parte do filme.)

DISTRIBUTIVE ADJECTIVES (ADJETIVOS DISTRIBUTIVOS)

Os adjetivos distributivos são quatro: *each*, *every*, *either*, *neither*. Fazem referência a indivíduos de um grupo. A concordância é feita com a 3ª pessoa do singular.

✱ *Each/Every* (cada)
Na maioria das vezes podem ocupar o lugar um do outro.

Each / Every *student is going to receive a gold medal.*
(Cada aluno receberá uma medalha de ouro.)
Each / Every *candidate wrote that in his/her paper.*
(Cada candidato escreveu isso em seu teste.)

Em alguns casos *each* enfatiza a individualidade e é mais usado para pequenos grupos (dois ou três). *Every* é usado para se referir a todos os membros de um grupo de mais de três.

Each *book costs twenty dollars.*
(Cada livro custa vinte dólares. > sugere um por um)
Every *house in the street is white.*
(Cada casa na rua é branca. > sugere todas elas)

Each pode fazer referência a apenas duas unidades e *every* não.

He was carrying a suitcase in **each** *hand.*
(Ele carregava uma valise em cada mão.)
Each hand **has** *five fingers.*
(Cada mão tem cinco dedos.)

✳ Either / Neither (um ou outro; qualquer um dos dois / nenhum dos dois)

Either dress suits me.

(Qualquer dos dois vestidos me serve.)

Today or tomorrow. Either day is fine.

(Hoje ou amanhã. Qualquer dia está bem.)

Neither girl is ready.

(Nenhuma das duas garotas está pronta.)

Neither answer was correct.

(Nenhuma das respostas estava correta.)

POSSESSIVE ADJECTIVES (ADJETIVOS POSSESSIVOS)

Possessivos são palavras como *my*, *mine*, *your*, *yours* etc. São usados para indicar o possuidor. Quando acompanham substantivos são adjetivos. Quando substituem substantivos são pronomes. Adjetivos e pronomes possessivos não são precedidos por artigos.

My car is cheaper than yours. (O meu carro é mais barato do que o seu.)

|adj.| |adv.|

Personal pronouns	Possessive adjectives	Possessive pronouns
I (eu)	*my* (meu, minha)	*mine* (o/a meu, minha)
you (tu, você)	*your* (teu, tua, seu, sua)	*yours* (o/a teu/seu, tua/sua)
he (ele)	*his* (dele)	*his* (o/a dele)
she (ela)	*her* (dela)	*hers* (o/a dela)
it (ele/a)	*its* (dele, dela)	*its* (o/a dele, dela)
we (nós)	*our* (nosso/a)	*ours* (o/a nosso/a)
you (vós, vocês)	*you* (vosso/a, seu, sua)	*yours* (o/a vosso/a, seu, sua)
they (eles/as)	*their* (deles/as)	*theirs* (o/a deles/as)

AGREEMENT (CONCORDÂNCIA)

✳ Adjetivos e pronomes possessivos concordam com o possuidor em gênero e número.

She	*loves*	**her** *father.*	(Ela ama seu pai.)
A dog	*loves*	**its** *owner.*	(Um cão ama seu dono.)
The Earth	*turns around*	**its** *axis.*	(A Terra gira ao redor de seu eixo.)
|possuidor|		| adj.|	

✳ Para demonstrar afetividade a países, navios e carros usam-se palavras do sexo feminino. Para animais domésticos, considera-se o sexo do animal.

Our dog is old. **His** *name is Thor.*
(Nosso cão é velho. Seu nome é Thor.)
I have a cat, **her** *name is Popcorn.*
(Tenho uma gata, seu nome é Popcorn.)
We have an old car. **Her** *color is red.*
(Temos um carro velho. Sua cor é vermelha.)

✳ Com palavras como *teacher*, *student*, *nurse* etc. a concordância é feita com *his/her* ou *their*.

Each student is bringing **his/her** *books.*
(Cada aluno está trazendo seus livros.)
A teacher must bring **their** *own book.*
(Um professor deve trazer seu próprio livro.)

GERUND (GERÚNDIO)[3]

Adjetivos possessivos **podem vir** junto a formas no gerúndio (verbo + *-ing)*.

> *Would you mind **my smoking** here?*
> (Você se importa que eu fume aqui?)
> *I appreciate **his fixing** the door.*
> (Agradeço por ele consertar a porta.)

PRACTICE

(respostas na pág. 130)

1. Classify the underlined words as **A** (adjective) or **P** (pronoun).

	A	P
1. *This apartment needs to be painted.*	✓	
2. *He lives in **this** house.*		
3. *How much is **that** bag?*		
4. *This book is mine. **That** is yours.*		
5. *Would you like **these** oranges?*		
6. *I am keeping **these** pencils.*		
7. *I am selling **those** books.*		
8. *Please give me **those** clothes.*		
9. *These shoes fit me very well. **Those** are too tight.*		
10. *This is the best day of my life.*		

2. Check the correct demonstratives and correct the wrong ones.

1. *Those brown dog always jumps over the fence.*	*that*
2. *That movie was hilarious.*	✓

---

3. Gerund – usado como substantivo: **Swimming** is healthy.
   Present Participle – usado como verbo ou adjetivo: He is **swimming**; Buy **swimming** clothes.

3. *I could eat all of these muffins.* _____
4. *Jeff loves those cookies.* _____
5. *I love these cake.* _____
6. *That dog is so adorable.* _____
7. *My son loves that muffins.* _____
8. *I couldn't sleep because that dogs were barking.* _____
9. *We bought that motorcycle.* _____
10. *Alice owns these old chair.* _____

3. **Underline only the demonstrative adjectives and translate the sentences.**

1. *I had never seen <u>such</u> a book.*
   <u>*Eu nunca tinha visto tal livro.*</u>

2. *This is a good car but I like that old banger.*

   _____.

3. *He bought these new socks and donated those to the team.*

   _____.

4. *I liked the former singer best.*

   _____.

5. *It was such a stupid story.*

   _____.

6. *This has been a difficult decade for the U.S. Presidency.*

   _____.

7. *We had never paid such taxes before.*

   _____.

8. *He sat on this seat.*

   _____.

9. *Even though I preferred those shirts, I bought these.*

   _____ .

10. *I find such people very boring.*

   _____ .

4. Choose the correct alternative.

1. *Either hotel (<u>is</u> /are) comfortable.*
2. *Neither cap (suit/suits) you.*
3. *I love her. I enjoyed (each/either) moment I spent with her.*
4. *I have (neither/every) album ever recorded by the Beatles.*
5. *It was an accident and neither (boys/boy) is responsible.*
6. *Every child in the world (deserves/deserve) affection.*
7. *— Which coat do you want, the blue or the black one?*
   — (Either/Every) coat will do, thanks a lot.
8. *Every society (has/have) its own rules.*
9. *Either (days/day) is suitable for me.*
10. *Neither girl (has/have) started elementary school. They are illiterate.*
11. *Each artist (sees/see) things differently.*
12. *The President gave each (soldier/soldiers) a medal.*
13. *Either title (are/is) appropriate, but I suggest the former.*
14. *He tells a lie (each/either) time he talks to me.*
15. *I liked (either/neither) film. They were both boring.*

5. Classify the possessives as **A** (adjective) or **P** (pronoun).

	A	P
1. *<u>Our</u> house is clean.*	____	____
2. *Roger and Carla are <u>our</u> friends.*	____	____
3. *Did that cat hurt <u>its</u> ear?*	____	____
4. *This book is <u>theirs</u>.*	____	____
5. *<u>Your</u> copybooks are in the lab.*	____	____
6. *These cars are <u>hers</u>.*	____	____

7. *What is __his__ name?* _____ _____
8. *These are __our__ books.* _____ _____
9. *This DVD isn't __yours__. It's __his__.* _____ _____
10. *Do you know __their__ parents?* _____ _____

6. Choose the correct adjective.

1. *Karen is from France. (__Her__ /His) husband is from Italy.*
2. *June and Alex are going to school. (His/Their) brother is going to the gym.*
3. *We study near here. (Ours/Our) school is fantastic.*
4. *Two girls didn't bring (their/her) books.*
5. *Although I don't like gray, (my/mine) car is gray.*
6. *Those boys are Brazilian but (theirs/their) family is from Japan.*
7. *Jessica likes (his/her) grandfather.*
8. *Charles likes singing with (his/her) sister.*
9. *My sister has sold (her/its) old bike.*
10. *Jeff and (his /her) mother are waiting for you.*
11. *Do you go to school with (your/yours) brother?*
12. *There is (my/mine) mother and (his/her) brother.*
13. *That dog buried (its/hers) bone under the tree.*
14. *Is Marco in (mine/his) bedroom?*
15. *My dog Fido hurt (hers/his) leg under the car.*

Interrogative, Quantitative and Descriptive Adjectives

Which is the **shortest** way?
I've bought **many green** apples.

BASICS

INTERROGATIVE ADJECTIVES (ADJETIVOS INTERROGATIVOS)

As palavras *what*, *which* e *whose* podem funcionar como interrogativos. São adjetivos quando antecedem substantivos. São usados para coisas, pessoas etc. e não variam de forma.

✱ *what* (que, qual)

É usado em perguntas genéricas; refere-se a um número ilimitado de coisas.

What time is the show?
(A que horas é o show?)
What color are her eyes?
(Qual a cor dos olhos dela?)
What book are you going to buy?
(Qual livro você vai comprar?)

✳ *which* (qual)

Refere-se a um número restrito de coisas; também usado para escolhas óbvias ou conhecidas.

Which hand do you write with?
(Com qual mão você escreve?)
Which side of the street do you live on?
(De qual lado da rua você mora?)
Which car did you sell, the blue one?
(Que carro você vendeu, o azul?)

✳ *whose* (de quem)

É usado para perguntar a quem algo pertence.

Whose books are these?
(De quem são estes livros?)
Whose sister is he?
(Ele é irmão de quem?)
Whose magazines are these?
(De quem são estas revistas?)

QUANTITATIVE ADJECTIVES (ADJETIVOS QUANTITATIVOS)[1]

Palavras como *some*, *any*, *much*, *many*, *full*, *enough* etc. fazem referência à quantidade de algo. Quando antecedem substantivos são adjetivos. Quando substituem substantivos são pronomes.

---

1. Outras denominações: **adjectives of number, of quantity, indefinites** etc.

*I bought **many** apples. **Some** are rotten.*

|adj.| |pron.|

(Comprei muitas maçãs. Algumas estão podres.)

Quantitativos mais comuns:

any (algum): *Is there any bread?* (Há algum pão?)
enough (suficiente): *He has enough money.* (Ele tem dinheiro suficiente.)
few (poucos): *Few people know him.* (Poucas pessoas o conhecem.)
full (cheio): *This box is full.* (Esta caixa está cheia.)
heavy (pesado): *There was a heavy rain today.*

(Houve uma chuva pesada hoje.)

little (pouco): *She drinks little coffee.* (Ela toma pouco café.)
many (muitos): *We have many cousins.* (Temos muitos primos.)
no (nenhum): *There is no rice for dinner.* (Não há arroz para o jantar.)
some (algum/uns): *I have eaten some cookies.* (Comi alguns bolinhos.)
two (dois): *I hurt two fingers.* (Feri dois dedos.)

Obs.:

✳ *some*

Usado em frases afirmativas, em pedidos, oferecimentos ou quando se espera uma resposta positiva.

***Some** students are tired.*
(Alguns alunos estão cansados.)
*Will you lend me **some** money?*
(Você pode me emprestar algum dinheiro?)

✳ *no*

Usado em frases negativas.

*There is **no** money left.*

(Não sobrou nenhum dinheiro.)

✳ *any*

Usado em frases interrogativas, negativas, com palavras de sentido negativo (never, rarely etc.), após *if* e *whether* ou com o significado de *qualquer*.

*Is there **any** money left?*

(Sobrou algum dinheiro?)

*There **isn't** any money left.*

(Não sobrou nenhum dinheiro.)

*He left **without** any money.*

(Ele saiu sem nenhum dinheiro.)

*I don't know **whether** there is any money left.*

(Não sei se sobrou algum dinheiro.)

*If you have **any** doubt, tell me.*

(Se tiver alguma dúvida, diga-me.)

***Any** schoolboy knows it.*

(Qualquer garoto sabe disso.)

✳ *enough*

Antes do substantivo, exerce a função de adjetivo; após adjetivo ou verbo, exerce a função de advérbio.

(adj.) *Do you have **enough** money for the tickets?*

(Você tem dinheiro suficiente para os ingressos?)

(adv.) *He was kind **enough** to help me.*

(Ele foi bondoso o suficiente para me ajudar.)

(adv.) *She worked **enough** to buy a car.*

(Ela trabalhou o suficiente para comprar um carro.)

Também são adjetivos quantitativos palavras como:

abundant, empty, extra, light, several, sparse, substantial, whole etc.
(abundante, vazio, extra, leve, vários, escasso, substancial, inteiro)

DESCRIPTIVE ADJECTIVES (ADJETIVOS DESCRITIVOS)[1]
(ver Order of Adjectives na pág. 35)

Palavras como *large, red, intelligent, long* etc. são adjetivos descritivos. Podem descrever opinião, cor, tamanho, som, gosto, toque, forma, qualidade, tempo, personalidade, idade etc.

*I make **monthly** trips to the Mall.*
(Faço idas mensais ao shopping.)
*She is a **pretty young** lady.*
(Ela é uma bela jovem senhora.)
*The **early** earth was **full** of **simple** molecules.*
(A terra primitiva era repleta de moléculas simples.)

É possível usar vários adjetivos para qualificar um substantivo. Nesse caso, a ordem dos adjetivos não é aleatória. Há uma sequência formal a ser seguida:

Opinião/ tamanho/ idade/ cor/ etc.

*He is a **courageous young** man.* (opinião, idade)
(Ele é um jovem corajoso.)
*That is a **nice ancient** bench.* (opinião, idade)
(Aquele é um belo banco antigo.)
*She has a **beautiful, long, red** scarf.* (opinião, tamanho, cor)
(Ela tem um lindo, longo cachecol vermelho.)

2. Outras denominações: **descriptive, qualifying, classifying adjectives** etc.

*I've got a **pretty large ancient white** house.*
(opinião, tamanho, idade, cor)

(Tenho uma linda, grande, antiga casa branca.)

PRACTICE

(respostas na pág. 131)

1. Rewrite the sentences. Use *which*.

1. *What language do you speak most fluently?*
<u>Which language do you speak most fluently: Spanish, German, or Italian?</u>

2. *What soccer team is the best?*

_____.

3. *What color is your book?*

_____.

4. *What direction do I go?*

_____.

5. *What color do you like best?*

_____.

2. Complete the sentences.

1. ___*What*___ *colors are there in a rainbow?*
2. _____ *books are these?*
3. "_____ *car is hers?" "The red one."*
4. _____ *pen is this? Is it John's?*
5. _____ *cake would you prefer?*
6. _____ *is the best road to take?*
7. _____ *river is that?*

8. "_____ car is yours?" "The blue car is mine."
9. _____ finger did you injure?
10. _____ photo is that one over there? Is it yours?
11. _____ day is it today?
12. _____ age is your grandma?
13. _____ is the depth of the lake?
14. _____ state is the largest?
15. _____ color is your cat?

3. Underline all quantitative adjectives.

1. I have <u>two</u> houses in London
2. She has many friends in Liverpool.
3. I have so few chances to meet my friends.
4. Several students are learning English.
5. He lost all his wealth.
6. We have little faith in the system.
7. Is that box full?
8. The meteorologists have predicted there will be sufficient rain this year.
9. We didn't have enough time to visit Paris.
10. Have you got any rice?
11. There is a substantial supply of food for winter.
12. Many rainfalls have disrupted life in India.
13. I have heard it numerous times.
14. There is enough bread for lunch.
15. Some people are irresponsible.

4. Underline the correct alternative.

1. There was not (<u>much</u> /some) time left to get the train.
2. We seldom have (any/few) doubt.
3. She ate the (sufficient/whole) apple.
4. I ate (some/two) rice.
5. There is (enough/full) water in the bucket.

6. There was (no/any) milk in the jug.
7. He has a (many/little) knowledge.
8. We got a (little/few) time to meet Paul.
9. You have (no/any) sense.
10. He was happy because he had sold (full/all) his pies.

5. Choose the correct alternatives to complete the text.

1. Half of all (cold/<u>fresh</u>) tomatoes in the U.S. come from Florida farms.
2. This region that feeds the country has a (dirty/enough) secret.
3. Working conditions there are (nice/terrible) .
4. The days are very (tall/hot).
5. Workers have to carry hundreds of (light/heavy) boxes every day.
6. They receive (little/empty) to no pay.

6. Complete the sentences with adjectives from the box.

> *famous   largest   expensive   Brazilian   first   first*

1. The _____*first*_____ radio transmission in Brazil went on the air on September, 1922.
2. Radios were _____ at that time.
3. Brazil's _____ shows were Cuban, adapted for _____ audiences.
4. The radionovela Right to be Born (Direito de Nascer), was considered the _____ success of all time. It went on the air in 1951.
5. The radio-actress Isis de Oliveira was one of the _____ names of Rádio Nacional do Rio de Janeiro between 1940 and 1960.

7. Rewrite the adjective in parentheses in the correct place.

1. (two) No _____*two*_____ zebras have _____ the same stripes.

2. (vocal) *The _____ giraffe has _____ no _____ cords.*

3. (rectangular) *_____ Goat's eyes have _____ pupils.*

4. (black) *A _____ zebra is white with _____ stripes.*

5. (Asian) *Happy, a female _____ elephant recognized herself in the _____ mirror.*

6. (favorite) *George Washington's _____ horse was named _____ Lexington.*

7. (sacred) *Ancient Egyptians believed that _____ cats were _____ animals .*

8. (powerful) *The ostrich's vigorous legs are _____ enough _____ to kill a man.*

9. (left-handed) *All polar _____ bears are _____ .*

10. (black) *A cat's _____ urine glows under a _____ light.*

11. (human) *Grizzly bears have long _____ claws about the length of a _____ finger.*

12. (vegetarian) *Cats cannot survive on a _____ diet _____ .*

13. (blowing) *Camels have three eyelids to protect themselves from _____ sand _____ .*

14. (different) *Chameleons can move their eyes in two _____ directions at the same _____ time.*

15. (Brown) *_____ eggs come from hens with red feathers and red ear lobes _____ .*

Order of Adjectives

Buy **some fresh** eggs.
I have a **good old blue Italian** car.

BASICS

A ordem dos adjetivos é algo bastante importante em inglês. Uma ordem fora do usual dá à frase um tom "estranho" facilmente percebido por nativos do idioma.

A tabela a seguir resume a ordem em que adjetivos em série devem ser colocados. É pouco comum o uso de mais de três ou quatro adjetivos para um substantivo. A longa frase foi construída apenas para exemplificar.

ADJECTIVE MASTER CHART

adjective[1]	example	sentence
1. articles, possessives, demonstratives	the, a, this, my,...	The
2. ordinal number	first, second...	first
3. quantity	one, much, some...	two
4. opinion, description	good, bad,...	good
5. size, height, length	big, small...	big
6. age, temperature	old, hot...	old
7. shape	round, square...	square
8. color	blue, brown...	brown
9. participle	known, amazing...	known
10. origin, location	Asian, Chinese...	Chinese
11. material	rock, wooden...	stone
12. purpose	sleeping, frying...	religious
noun	man, house...	**buildings**

1. Artigos, possessivos, demonstrativos e quantitativos também recebem a denominação de **determiners**. Adjetivos descritivos e advérbios também recebem a denominação de **modifiers**.

Observe:

a small white **house**
(uma pequena casa branca)
those five good **books**
(aqueles cinco bons livros)
an old traveling **salesman**
(o velho vendedor ambulante)
the first cold **days**
(os primeiros dias frios)
the last two **months**
(os últimos dois meses)
those old dilapidated brick **houses**
(aquelas velhas e dilapidadas casas de tijolo)
a small, dark brown, leather **case**
(um pequeno estojo marrom escuro de couro)

Nota: para adjetivos do mesmo tipo use a ordem que preferir.

I have a **gentle**, **kind**, **funny** *roommate.* (opinion)
(Tenho um colega de quarto gentil, bondoso e engraçado.)

PUNCTUATION (PONTUAÇÃO)

* Adjetivos após substantivos > separar por *and*.

    The clothes were clean **and** *dry.*
    (As roupas estavam limpas e secas.)
    The dancers were tall, thin **and** *graceful.*
    (As bailarinas eram altas, magras e graciosas.)

* Adjetivos de significados diferentes > não precisam de vírgulas

    It was a bright happy **day**.
    (Era um dia luminoso e feliz.)

✱ Quando dois adjetivos puderem ser separados pela palavra *and*, podem ser separados por vírgula.

The critics said it was a profound, controversial, amazing story.
(Os críticos disseram que era uma história profunda, controversa e notável.)

PRACTICE

(respostas na pág. 133)

1. Match the sentence parts.

A

1. *They will demolish those* <u>*five red brick*</u> *houses.* (*b*)
2. *He has bought* _____ *trousers.* ( )
3. *Did you buy that* _____ *table?* ( )
4. *She loves blue. Is she wearing her* _____ *dress?* ( )
5. *The girls need* _____ *balls for that activity.* ( )

a. *blue silk*
b. *five red brick*
c. *slim new Italian*
d. *square, gray, stone*
e. *five small paper*

B

6. *There are* <u>*two beautiful*</u> *dresses in her closet.* (*e*)
7. *He invited that* _____ *lady to dinner.* ( )
8. *I've booked that* _____ *table on the corner.* ( )
9. *She sells* _____ *cookies.* ( )
10. *What do you plan to do with these* _____ *wine bottles?* ( )

a. *gentle young*
b. *four empty*
c. *delicious chocolate*
d. *big round*
e. *two beautiful*

C

11. *We are waiting for the* <u>three last</u> *people to arrive.*   (*e*)
12. *Give her that _____ French scarf.*   (   )
13. *How about some _____ beer?*   (   )
14. *A _____ dog is sleeping under my car.*   (   )
15. *He is selling _____ typewriters.*   (   )

a. *cold English*
b. *beautiful green*
c. *old repaired*
d. *fat black*
e. *three last*

2. Check the correct adjective order.

1. *There are _____ houses in our street.*
   ☑ *three empty*
   ☐ *empty three*

2. *She lives in _____ Victorian cottage.*
   ☐ *a pretty, old*
   ☐ *an old, pretty*

3. *She wants to become _____ star.*
   ☐ *a singing international*
   ☐ *an international singing*

4. *Her neighbor is* _____ *Dutch man*
   - ☐ *an old, interesting*
   - ☐ *an interesting, old*

5. *He drives* _____ *German car.*
   - ☐ *a big, expensive*
   - ☐ *an expensive, big*

6. *We use* _____ *ingredients.*
   - ☐ *fresh British*
   - ☐ *British fresh*

7. *My husband is* _____ *man.*
   - ☐ *a big, dark-haired*
   - ☐ *a dark-haired, big*

8. *I love* _____ *Spanish wine.*
   - ☐ *fine, old*
   - ☐ *old, fine*

9. *The* _____ *dog slept under the couch.*
   - ☐ *black, old, big*
   - ☐ *big, old, black*

10. *We saw a nice round* _____ *house.*
    - ☐ *brick old white*
    - ☐ *old white brick*

11. *We gave him* _____ *clock.*
    - ☐ *a wonderful old Italian*
    - ☐ *an old wonderful Italian*

12. *Archeologists have found* _____ *animal bones.*
    - ☐ *large, prehistoric*
    - ☐ *prehistoric, large*

39

13. *Give me the* _____ *box.*
- ☐ *big square blue*
- ☐ *square big blue*

14. *He prefers* _____ *leather furniture.*
- ☐ *Italian, black*
- ☐ *black, Italian*

15. *I have* _____ *brothers.*
- ☐ *three little*
- ☐ *little three*

3. Write **C** (for correct) or **I** (for incorrect sentences).

1. *The colorful lionfish is covered with fins that inject poison.* _____
2. *Centuries ago books were made of wood and were heavys.* _____
3. *The human heart creates enough pressure to pump blood 9 meters.* _____
4. *A normal cow's stomach has four compartments.* _____
5. *German Shepherds bite humans more than any other breed of dog.* _____
6. *Although considered a pest, a rat is highly intelligent.* _____
7. *Dolphins are extremely social beings and have language "sophisticated".* _____
8. *Elisha Otis invented the brake used in elevators modern.* _____
9. *She's a calm very person.* _____
10. *DDT was a very effective insecticide.* _____
11. *Humans are creative. We have language and use it to express complex ideas.* _____
12. *Ancients Japanese thought that earthquakes were caused by a giant spider living under the earth.* _____
13. *Howler monkeys are the noisiests land animals.* _____
14. *The hummingbird is the only animal that can fly backwards.* _____
15. *The general atmosphere of the conference was great.* _____

4. Read the sentences about London. Write **C** (for correct) and **I** (for incorrect sentences).

1. *May: The first weekend sees the arrival of London Wonderground on the South Bank.* _____
2. *The British Library presents its major summer exhibition.* _____
3. *Modern music is at the forefront of A Scream and an Outrage at the Barbican.* _____
4. *Singer Italian Zucchero performs at the Royal Albert Hall on Wednesday.* _____
5. *May is a sporting big month in London with a number of football, rugby and cricket tournaments.* _____
6. *The Investec Derby Festival takes place on the last weekend of the month.* _____

Form of Adjectives

He knows **interesting** stories.
I love **Italian** painters.

BASICS

Além de palavras como *big*, *beautiful*, *expensive*, *thin* etc. que são facilmente identificadas como adjetivos, muitas outras palavras podem exercer tal função.

Observe.

* particípios: *amusing, interesting, excited*
* palavras formadas pela adição de afixos: *Irish, joyful, cloudy*
* palavras compostas: *good-looking, well-dressed, race horse*

PRESENT AND PAST PARTICIPLE (PARTICÍPIO PRESENTE E PASSADO)[1]

O particípio presente (verbo + -ing) e o particípio passado (verbo + -ed) podem ser usados como adjetivos.

-ing:	*amus**ing***	*disgust**ing***	*fascinat**ing***
(tem a ação)	engraçado	repugnante	fascinante

-ed:	*excit**ed***	*fascinat**ed***	*disappoint**ed***
(afetado pela ação)	entusiasmado	fascinado	decepcionado

---

1. O Particípio Presente funciona como adjetivo. Pode ser confundido com o Gerúndio, usado na formação dos tempos Contínuos. Ex: **The smiling girl; The girl is smiling.**
O Particípio Passado funciona como adjetivo. Pode ser confundido com o passado simples de verbos. Ex: **The parked car; I parked a car.**

*That was an interest**ing** film.*

(Foi um filme interessante.)

*He is an interest**ed** person.*

(Ele é uma pessoa interessada.)

*That is an amus**ing** story.*

(Essa é uma história divertida.)

*This is an amus**ed** child.*

(Esta é uma criança entretida.)

AFFIXES (AFIXOS)

É possível formar adjetivos a partir de verbos, substantivos, advérbios ou mesmo de adjetivos através do acréscimo de afixos (prefixos ou sufixos).

✳ suffixes (sufixos)

-able/-ible:	*drink**able***	*wash**able***	*fashion**able***
(tem a qualidade)	bebível	lavável	na moda

-al/-ial/-ical:	*accident**al***	*influent**ial***	*nation**al***
(tem o resultado)	acidental	influente	nacional

-an/-ese/-ish:	*Indi**an***	*Nepal**ese***	*Ir**ish***
(tem a origem)	indiano	nepalês	irlandês

-ed:	*beard**ed***	*talent**ed***	*wood**ed***
(tem a característica)	barbudo	talentoso	arborizado

-ent:	*absorb**ent***	*differ**ent***	*persist**ent***
(é ou faz)	absorvente	diferente	persistente

-ful:	*beauti**ful***	*color**ful***	*pain**ful***
(tem a qualidade; cheio)	belo	colorido	doloroso

-ic: (sobre, a respeito)	*artistic* artístico	*democratic* democrático	*poetic* poético
-ish: (semelhante a; um tanto)	*childish* infantil	*foolish* insensato	*bluish* azulado
-ive: (tende a)	*creative* criativo	*productive* produtivo	*progressive* progressivo
-less: (sem)	*colorless* incolor	*homeless* sem-teto	*restless* inquieto
-like: (como)	*childlike* infantil	*prison-like* prisional	*businesslike* metódico
-ly: (tem a qualidade)	*daily* diário	*motherly* maternal	*friendly* amigável
-ous: (tem a característica)	*mountainous* montanhoso	*desirous* desejoso	*dangerous* perigoso
-y: (tem a qualidade; cheio)	*cloudy* nublado	*hairy* cabeludo	*sandy* arenoso

✳ **prefixes** (prefixos)

dis-, il-, im-, in-, ir-, un-: (sem; o oposto de)	*disorganized* desorganizado *inactive* inativo	*illegal* ilegal *irregular* irregular	*impatient* impaciente *unsafe* inseguro
super-; ultra-; sub-: (mais do que; além de; abaixo)	*supernatural* supernatural	*ultrasound* ultrassom	*subconscious* subconsciente

over-; hyper-:	**over**busy	**over**dressed	**hyper**active
(excessivo; extremo)	ocupado demais	vestido em excesso	hiperativo

uni-, mono-; bi-:	**uni**lateral	**mono**lingual	**bi**colored
(um; dois)	unilateral	monolíngue	bicolor

*The day is cloud**y**.*

(O dia está nublado.)

*That was a pain**ful** solution.*

(Foi uma solução dolorosa.)

*The couple is child**less**.*

(O casal é sem filhos.)

*Is this water drink**able**?*

(Essa água é potável?)

*He is a talent**ed** young man.*

(Ele é um jovem talentoso.)

*It is a very **ir**regular action.*

(É uma ação muito irregular.)

*Dads can show some mother**ly** instincts.*

(Pais podem mostrar instintos maternais.)

*This is just a friend**ly** reminder.*

(É apenas um lembrete amigável.)

COMPOUND ADJECTIVES (ADJETIVOS COMPOSTOS)

É possível unir diferentes classes de palavras para formar **compound adjectives**. Se causam ambiguidade quando ligados aos substantivos, recebem hífen.

Veja algumas das junções possíveis.

adjective/ adverb/ noun +	present or/ past participle	*good-looking* (bonito)	*heart-breaking* (doloroso)
		cold-blooded (sangue frio)	*handmade* (feito à mão)
adjective +	adjective/ noun/ noun -ed	*dark-blue* (azul-escuro)	*light-brown* (marrom-claro)
		fast-food (comida rápida)	*round-table* (de mesa-redonda)
		blue-eyed (de olhos azuis)	*bad-tempered* (de mau temperamento)
noun +	noun/ adjective	*race boats[2]* (barcos de corrida)	*waterproof* (à prova de água)
		part-time (meio-período)	*left-hand* (da mão esquerda)
adverb +	adjective	*highly-respectable* (muito estimado)	*fiercely-competitive* (intensamente competitivo)
verb +	preposition	*stick-on* (afixado)	*drive-in* (de carro)
others +	others	*down-to-earth* (com os pés no chão)	*one-way* (unidirecional)
		two-year-old (de dois anos)	*second-hand* (de segunda-mão)

Veja alguns exemplos interessantes

well-known actor
(um ator bem conhecido)

six-year-old cat
(suéter azul-escuro)

middle-aged lady
(senhora de meia-idade)

dark-blue sweater
(gato de seis anos)

2. Plural - 1) nas palavras compostas, apenas o substantivo real pode ir para o plural: shoe**laces**, boat **races**; 2) palavras originalmente terminadas por –s mantém o –s: **clothes** shops, **sports** suit, **news** reporter.

life-changing adventure
(aventura transformadora)

round-table discussion
(mesa-redonda; conversa)

four-wheel drive
(tração nas quatro rodas)

thirty-third part
(trigésima-terceira parte)

shorter-term loan
(empréstimo de prazo menor)

Anglo-Indian book
(livro anglo-indiano)

PRACTICE

(respostas na pág. 134)

1. Add *-ful* and *-less* to create adjectives. Translate the new words.

1. **care** (cuidado)	*care**ful*** (cuidadoso)	*care**less*** (descuidado)
2. **color** (cor)		
3. **doubt** (dúvida)		
4. **fear** (medo)		
5. **force** (força)		
6. **fruit** (fruto)		
7. **power** (potência)		
8. **taste** (sabor)		

2. Add *-able* to create adjectives. Translate the new words.

1. **accept** (aceitar)	*accept**able*** (aceitável)
2. **bear** (suportar)	
3. **believe** (crer)	
4. **compare** (comparar)	
5. **desire** (desejar)	
6. **drink** (beber)	
7. **predict** (prever)	
8. **wash** (lavar)	

3. Add *-ive* to create adjectives. Translate the new words.

1. *attract* (atrair)	*attractive* (atrativo)
2. *construct* (construir)	
3. *expand* (expandir)	
4. *expend* (gastar)	
5. *explode* (explodir)	
6. *instruct* (instruir)	
7. *offend* (ofender)	
8. *talk* (falar)	

4. Add the correct suffix to create new adjectives.

noun	adjective
accident	*accidental*
danger	
length	
star	
wind	
adjective	**adjective**
comic	*comical*
correct	
red	
elder	

5. Choose the correct participles to complete the sentences.

1. *The kids were* |*frightening* *because they had seen a rat.*
   | *frightened*

2. *She said that babysitting was an* | *exhausting* *task.*
   | *exhausted*

3. I get | boring   when I go to formal events.
        | bored

4. Today, the news on TV were | depressing.
                                         | depressed.

5. Your kid was | fascinating   by the book I gave him.
               | fascinated

6. The concert was | exciting,   wasn't it?
                | excited

6. Complete the sentences with the correct adjectives.

> red-eyed   long-lasting   old-fashioned   well-behaved
> low-cost   brightly-lit   cold-blooded

1. I have a _well-behaved_ dog.
2. They draw a _____ monster.
3. She loves a _____ apartment.
4. We signed a _____ agreement.
5. My parents live in an _____ house.
6. He is a _____ murderer.
7. In the future we will have _____ electric vehicles.

7. Rewrite the expressions. Follow the example.

1. A cat that is six years old is
   a six-year-old cat

2. An adventure that was life changing is

   _____

3. *A process that requires decision making is*

_____

4. *The man who is narrow minded is*

_____

5. *A man who's got black hair is*

_____

6. *A baby who is six months old is*

_____

7. *A person who works part time is*

_____

8. Write the correct adjective. Follow the example.

1. *A horse that runs in races is a* — *race horse*
2. *A race for horses is a* — *horse race*
3. *A story about love is a* _____
4. *A table for playing billiards is a* _____
5. *A race for boats is a* _____
6. *An exhibition for computers is a* _____
7. *A shop that sells clothes is a* _____
8. *Shoes for playing tennis are* _____
9. *Balls for playing golf are* _____
10. *Trainers for athletics are* _____
11. *Clubs for sports are* _____
12. *A department for accounts is an* _____
13. *A teacher for English is an* _____
14. *A writer of the article is an* _____
15. *A picnic on Sunday is a* _____
16. *A dress for a wedding is a* _____
17. *An editor for the news is a* _____
18. *Food for dog is* _____

19. *Food for dog that is delicious is* _____

20. *A man that sells car is a* _____

21. *A man that sells car and is honest is an* _____

22. *A coach for a team of football is a* _____

23. *A jar for coffee is a* _____

24. *A jar for coffee that is empty is an* _____

25. *A centre for conventions is a* _____

Adverbs

They are **always** tired.
She got up **quickly**.

BASICS

Advérbios são palavras como *happily*, *sadly*, *now*, *here* etc. Um grande número é formado pelo acréscimo do sufixo *-ly*. Advérbios acrescentam sentido a adjetivos, verbos, outros advérbios ou uma frase inteira, modificando-os.

Podem indicar lugar, tempo, modo, intensidade, dúvida, negação e afirmação, respondendo a indagações como:

How?   *Where?*   *When?*   *How often?*   *Why?*

*He paid **extremely** high prices.* (Ele pagou preços extremamente altos.)
　　　　　　　　 |adj.

*She smiled **shyly**.* (Ela sorriu timidamente.)
　　 |v.

*Kree danced **very** badly.* (Kree dançou muito mal.)
　　　　　　　 |adv.

***Fortunately**, nobody noticed.* (Felizmente, ninguém notou.)
　　　　　　　|sentence

***Certainly**, nobody knew the answer.* (Certamente, ninguém sabia a resposta.)

KINDS[1] OF ADVERBS (TIPOS DE ADVÉRBIOS)

(ver Adverb List na pág. 124)

Como os advérbios constituem uma classe muito heterogênea de palavras, torna-se difícil atribuir-lhes uma classificação uniforme. Podem receber classificações como: **simples** *(just, only, well, etc.)*, **compostos** *(somehow, hereby etc.)* e **derivados** *(safely, clockwise, northwards etc.)* ou outras bastante específicas.

De modo geral, podemos dizer que há advérbios de:

manner (modo) – informa sobre o modo como a ação ocorre:
slowly, eagerly, well, fast , hard, badly etc.
(lentamente, ansiosamente, bem, rapidamente, duramente, mal)

place (lugar) – informa sobre o local em que a ação ocorre.
here, outside, anywhere, home, out, upstairs etc.
(aqui, do lado de fora, qualquer lugar, casa, fora, andar de cima)

time (tempo) – informa sobre o tempo em que a ação ocorre.
now, then, soon, after, finally, recently etc.
(agora, então, logo, após, finalmente, recentemente)

degree, intensity, quantity (grau, intensidade, quantidade) – informa sobre a intensidade da ação ou sua quantidade.
very, quite, completely, much, fully, enough etc.
(muito, inteiramente, completamente, muito, completamente, suficientemente)

frequency (frequência) – informa com que frequência a ação ocorre.
never, always, often, daily, monthly, seldom etc.
(nunca, sempre, frequentemente, diariamente, mensalmente, raramente)

---

1. Também funcionam como advérbio: orações infinitivas, orações e expressões adverbiais: **I ran to see her; When this class is over,...; ...by train; ...to the movies; ...in the morning; ...as often as possible** etc.

*She speaks **slowly**.*

(Ela fala lentamente.)

*He ran **fast** to catch the bus.*

(Ele correu rapidamente para pegar o ônibus.)

*You drive **well**.*

(Você dirige bem.)

*He wants to go **upstairs**.*

(Ele quer ir para o piso superior.)

*Let's leave **now**.*

(Vamos sair agora.)

*He is **quite** capable of doing the task.*

(Ele é inteiramente capaz de fazer a tarefa.)

*We study French **daily**.*

(Estudamos Francês diariamente.)

COMPLEMENTARY

LINKING VERBS[2] (VERBOS DE LIGAÇÃO)

Verbos de ligação como *look*, *smell*, *taste*, *feel* etc., que são geralmente usados com adjetivos, mudam de significado quando usados com advérbios[3].

verb	adjective	adverb
feel	*I feel good.* (Eu me sinto bem.)	*This shirt feels well.* (Esta camisa é agradável ao toque.)
look	*She looks confident.* (Ela parece confiante.)	*She looked confidently at me.* (Ela olhou confiante para mim.)
smell	*The cake smells good.* (O bolo cheira bem.)	*Joe can smell well.* (Joe tem bom olfato.)
taste	*This pie tastes good.* (Esta torta tem gosto bom.)	*Jack tastes well.* (Jack tem bom paladar.)

2. Linking verbs: be, become, get, keep, make, appear, seem, look, smell, sound, taste, feel, grow, remain, prove, stay and turn. 3. Quando a palavra descreve a ação do verbo, é um advérbio. Quando descreve o sujeito, é um adjetivo.

MULTIPLE FUNCTIONS (MÚLTIPLAS FUNÇÕES)

Palavras como *fast*, *hard*, *early*, *friendly*, *well* etc. podem funcionar como adjetivo e advérbio.

(ver Common Mistakes na pág. 101)

adjective

*This is a **fast** car.*

(Este é um carro rápido.)

*That was a **hard** winter.*

(Foi um inverno difícil.)

*He is **well**.*

(Ele está bem. = saúde)

adverb

*She worked **fast**.*

(Ela trabalhou rapidamente.)

*They worked **hard**.*

(Eles trabalharam duro.)

*He behaved **well**.*

(Ele se comportou bem.)

Palavras como *when*, *where* e *why* podem funcionar como advérbio interrogativo e advérbio relativo.

***When** do you jog?*

(Quando você corre?)

***Where** does he live?*

(Onde ele mora?)

***Why** is she sad?*

(Porque ela está triste?)

*I remember the day **when** he arrived.*

(Lembro-me do dia que ele morreu.)

*That is the house **where** he lived.*

(Aquela é a casa onde ele viveu.)

*I don't know the reason **why** he left.*

(Não sei a razão pela qual ele saiu.)

How pode funcionar como advérbio interrogativo e conjunção.

***How** did they go?*

(Como eles foram?)

***How** tall is he?*

(Quão alto ele é?)

***How often** do you see him?*

(Com que frequência você o vê?)

*I asked **how** I could help.*

(Perguntei como poderia ajudar.)

*He didn't know **how** to do it.*

(Ele não sabia como fazê-lo.)

Tanto os advérbios interrogativos quanto os relativos podem ser substituídos por outras formas:

interrogative	relative
when *> at what time*	***when*** *> in/on which*
where *> in what place*	***where*** *> in/at which*
why *> for what reason*	***why*** *> for which*

***When**/At what time does it start?*

(Quando/A que horas começa?)

***Where**/In what place can I meet her?*

(Onde/Em que lugar posso encontrá-la?)

***Why**/For what reason did you invite him?*

(Porque/Por qual razão o convidou?)

*I remember the day **when**/on which he died.*

(Lembro-me do dia em que/no qual ele morreu.)

*I know the place **where**/at which he lives.*

(Conheço o local onde/no qual ele mora.)

*I know the reason **why**/for which he left.*

(Sei o porquê/a razão pela qual ele saiu.)

PRACTICE

(respostas na pág. 136)

1. Answer the questions. Use the adverbs in parentheses.

1. *How does he drive?*
(fast) <u>He drives fast.</u>

2. *Where did she go yesterday?*
(to school) _____

3. *When were you born?*
(in June) _____

4. *How often does she drink coffee?*
(every morning) _____

5. *How well does he speak English?*
(badly) _____

2. Classify the underlined adverbs as **M** *(manner)*, **P** *(place)*, **T** *(time)*,
F *(frequency)* or **D** *(degree)*.

1. *We <u>often</u> eat chicken for dinner.*   <u> F </u>
2. *Drive <u>slowly</u>, please.*   _____
3. *I had a nice party <u>yesterday</u>.*   _____
4. *Drop me a line when you get <u>there</u>.*   _____
5. *She has been to London <u>many times</u>.*   _____
6. *Let's leave <u>before</u> lunch.*   _____
7. *I am <u>usually</u> lucky at cards.*   _____
8. *We are <u>completely</u> lost.*   _____
9. *I saw her <u>this morning</u>.*   _____
10. *She received him <u>coldly</u>.*   _____
11. *Stay <u>here</u> until I am back.*   _____
12. *They went out of the room <u>quickly</u>.*   _____

13. *I talked to him __yesterday__.* ———
14. *Are the dogs __inside__ the kitchen?* ———
15. *She is __very__ beautiful.* ———

3. Choose the correct adverb.

1. *They played tennis very (today/__badly__).*
2. *I answered the questions (easily/out).*
3. *The music played (softly/here).*
4. *The man was (evidently/today) drunk.*
5. *You can (outside/easily) open this tin.*
6. *The man said that his work was (well/up) done.*
7. *Peter (never/just) gets angry.*
8. *We heard it (only/perfectly).*
9. *She worked (carefully/rather) with the sick child.*
10. *He (often/before) listens to the radio.*
11. *If you are poor, you have to be (fast/really) smart to get rich.*
12. *They (rarely/here) spend a day at the beach.*
13. *We play tennis (once/fully) a week.*
14. *He ran (comfortably/upstairs) to close the windows.*
15. *Go (abroad/straight) ahead and turn right at the corner.*

4. Underline the adverbs.

1. *The Stewarts live __abroad__.*
2. *Gary is really handsome.*
3. *He drives extremely fast.*
4. *That was extremely kind of you.*
5. *Obviously, they can't know everything.*
6. *My sister drives incredibly slowly.*
7. *Honestly, do you think he will get it?*
8. *We have often told them not to do that.*
9. *Has he come late?*
10. *She only ate bread.*

11. *Our teacher is angry. She shouts angrily.*
12. *Ted is usually very calm.*
13. *I can learn things fast.*
14. *He is a quiet man. He does his things quietly.*
15. *They were playing the guitar happily.*

5. Choose the correct relative adverb.

1. *That is the church (when/**where**) they got married.*
2. *May is the month (when/why) people buy presents to their moms.*
3. *I don't know the reason (where/why) he is studying German.*
4. *This is the street (how/where) I saw the thieves.*
5. *The day (why/when) I got married was rainy.*
6. *Christmas is a time (when/how) you get homesick.*
7. *The only place (where/how) success comes before work is in the dictionary.*
8. *An amusement park is a place (where/when) you can enjoy yourself.*
9. *Nobody knows the reason (how/why) he sold his houses.*
10. *Japan is one of the countries (when/where) people drive on the left.*

6. Complete with the correct alternative.

1. *wrongly – enough – carefully*
   *The turkey was named for what was _____**wrongly**_____ thought to be its country of origin.*

2. *hard – approximately – lately*
   It takes a lobster _____ seven years to grow to be one pound.

3. *since – happily – frequently*
   Dolphins sleep at night below the surface of the water. They _____ rise to the surface for air.

4. *enough – nearly – slowly*
   A cow gives _____ 200,000 glasses of milk in her lifetime.

5. *fast – nowhere – properly*
   A flamingo can't eat _____ unless its head is upside down.

6. *there – after – always*
   Bats _____ turn left when exiting a cave.

7. *well – good – badly*
   Dogs rely on their noses as they can smell extremely _____.

8. *easily – recently – monthly*
   Chimpanzees can _____ create and use tools.

9. *usually – often – highly*
   Although considered a pest, a rat _____ intelligent

10. *well – seldom – yearly*
    $1.5 billion is spent on pet food _____ . This is four times the amount spent on baby food.

Position and Order of Adverbs

She got up **slowly**.
She got up **slowly yesterday**.

BASICS

POSITION (POSIÇÃO)

De modo geral, há três posições principais que advérbios ou expressões adverbiais ocupam em uma frase.

início:	*Yesterday I saw him.*	> antes do sujeito
fim:	*I saw him **yesterday**.*	> no final da frase
meio:	*I **seldom** meet him.*	> entre sujeito e verbo
	*I can **often** see him.*	> entre verbo auxiliar e principal
	*I have a **very** fast car.*	> entre verbo e adjetivo
	*He was **usually** tired.*	> após verbo to be

A posição de advérbios nas frases depende da quantidade e do tipo dos advérbios presentes.

One Adverb (Um Advérbio)
Observe as possibilidades em frases contendo apenas um advérbio.[1]

---

1. Também funcionam como advérbio: orações infinitivas, orações e expressões adverbiais como: **I ran to see her; When this class is over, ...; ...by train; ...to the movies; ...in the morning; ...as often as possible** etc.

✳ Manner or place

após obj. dir. ou verbo:
*He drove the car **carefully**.*

(Ele dirigiu o carro cuidadosamente.)

*He drove **silently**.*

(Ele dirigiu silenciosamente.)

*She studied the lesson **here**.*

(Ela estudou a lição aqui.)

*She studied **there**.*

(Ela estudou lá.)

✳ Time

Início ou fim da frase:
***Yesterday** I saw him. / I saw him **yesterday**.*

(Eu o vi ontem.)

✳ Frequency

Início ou fim da frase:
***Sometimes** he goes to museums. / He goes to museums **sometimes**.*

(Ele vai a museus às vezes.)

antes do verbo principal:
*I **often** swim in the morning.*

(Frequentemente nado de manhã.)

*Do you **always** eat in a restaurant?*

(Você sempre come em um restaurante?)

*He could **never** speak.*

(Ele nunca podia falar.)

*I **always** can.*

(Eu sempre posso.)

Após verbo to be:
*He is **usually** late.*

(Ele geralmente está atrasado.)

Obs.: antes de used to:
*I **always** used to see him at school.*

(Eu costumava vê-lo sempre na escola.)

✳ Degree

Antes da palavra que modifica:
*He works **too** well[2].*

(Ele trabalha bem demais.)

*This book is **quite** good.*

(Este livro é bastante bom.)

*She can **almost** read.*

(Ela quase consegue ler.)

COMPLEMENTARY

ORDER OF ADVERBS (ORDEM DOS ADVÉRBIOS)

Two Adverbs (Dois Advérbios)
Com dois advérbios presentes, use a ordem a seguir.

✳ Manner – Time:
*I worked **harder** yesterday.*

(Trabalhei mais pesado ontem.)

✳ Place – Time:
*He arrived **here** late.*

(Ele chegou aqui tarde.)

2. Well: ver Common Mistakes na pág. 101.

* **Place – Manner:**
*She left **there** quickly.*

(Ela saiu de lá rapidamente.)

Three Adverbs or More (Três Advérbios ou Mais)

Quando há vários advérbios na mesma frase, a posição mais comum é no final da frase, na ordem: **Manner – Place – Time**.

A tabela resume a ordem para advérbios em série. As frases longas foram construídas apenas para exemplificar. O uso de muitos advérbios em uma mesma frase pode dificultar a compreensão.

ADVERB MASTER CHART [3]

subj./v.	Manner	Place	Frequency	Time	other
I sing	*happily*	*in my room*	*every day*	*in the morning.*	—
He runs	*quickly*	*around the lake*	*usually*	*after dinner.*	—
She walks	*slowly*	*into town*	*weekly*	*before lunch*	*to pay the bills.*

He danced well there.

(Eles dançaram bem lá.)

They work hard at home twice a week in the afternoon.

(Eles trabalham duramente em casa duas vezes por semana à tarde.)

I studied peacefully in the library yesterday.

(Ela estudou tranquilamente na biblioteca ontem.)

They quickly joined their group for dinner.

(Eles rapidamente juntaram-se ao seu grupo para o jantar.)

---

3. Adverbs of Degree não fazem parte da tabela pois são colocados imediatamente antes da palavra que modificam.

Notes:

✳ Expressões do mesmo tipo > a mais específica vem antes.
*I was born **in a brick house**, northern Nebraska.*
(Nasci em uma casa de tijolos, ao norte de Nebrasca.)
*He was born **at 1:00 p.m.** on New Year's Eve in 1952.*
(Ele nasceu à 1:00 da tarde na véspera do Ano Novo em 1952.)

✳ Expressões curtas > antecedem as longas
*I take a short walk **before breakfast** every day of my life.*
(Faço uma caminhada curta antes do café da manhã todos os dias de minha vida.)

✳ Ênfase > advérbio no início da frase
***Slowly** she got up.*
(Lentamente ela se levantou.)

✳ Para: inversão, ***only***, ***too***, ***enough***, ***yet***, ***still***, ***rather*** etc... (ver *Common Mistakes*)

PRACTICE

(respostas na pág. 137)

1. Write the adverbs of manner in the correct sentences.

well   dangerously   nicely   fast   easily   quietly

1. *Those guys drive* <u>dangerously</u> .
2. *My children behaved* _____ *during the ceremony.*
3. *How can you swim so* _____ ?
4. *Paul said that I speak English* _____ .
5. *She moved* _____ *around the room not to disturb the baby.*
6. *I could* _____ *find the way to the Central Park.*

2. Write the adverbs of place in the correct sentences.

> *downstairs   upstairs   outside   nearby   somewhere   there*

1. *The children are __outside__ , in the backyard.*
2. *Mom is _____ in the kitchen.*
3. *Your skate is _____ in the garage. Go look for it.*
4. *My bedroom is _____ close to the bathroom.*
5. *The bank is _____ , just a block to the north.*
6. *Can you go _____ with me?*

3. Write the adverbs of time in the correct sentences.

> *during   lately   next   for   already   yesterday*

1. *We are going to Italy __next__ summer.*
2. *He has waited for you _____ twenty minutes.*
3. *He fell asleep _____ the show. What a shame!*
4. *I haven't seen your sister _____ . How is she?*
5. *Jill has _____ arrived.*
6. *They went to the Zoo _____ after breakfast.*

4. Place the adverbs with the verbs.

1. *We go to the movies on Sundays. (sometimes)*
   We sometimes go to the movies on Sundays.

2. *It is hot in Brazil in January. (always)*

   _____ .

3. *It snows in October. (never)*

   _____ .

4. *I meet my brother on weekends. (seldom)*

_____ .

5. *Grandma sleeps after lunch. (usually)*

_____ .

6. *I have been to London because my brother lives there. (often)*

_____ .

5. Rewrite the sentences and place the adverbs correctly.

1. *The man drove badly. (really)*
<u>*The man drove really badly.*</u>

2. *The dentist is. (upstairs)*

_____ .

3. *I walk my dog. (seldom)*

_____ .

4. *The water was cold. (extremely)*

_____ .

5. *My sister is beautiful. (very)*

_____ .

6. *Grandma can hear. (well)*

_____ .

7. *I have seen you. (never)*

_____ .

8. *They enjoyed the play. (immensely)*

_____ .

9. *We agree with you. (entirely)*

_____ .

10. *We were in London. (last month)*

_____ .

6. Check all possible positions for the words in parentheses.

1. *patiently:* ☑ *She waited* ☑ .
2. *in winter: We* ☐ *don't swim* ☐ .
3. *completely:* ☐ *They are* ☐ *exhausted from the trip* ☐ .
4. *always: My brother* ☐ *plays* ☐ *the flute in the morning.*
5. *slowly: He* ☐ *walked* ☐ .
6. *too: You are* ☐ *young to drive* ☐ .
7. *there: I saw* ☐ *you* ☐ .
8. *quite: He drove* ☐ *dangerously* ☐ .
9. *very: She* ☐ *was* ☐ *sad.*
10. *fluently: I speak* ☐ *English* ☐ .

7. Rewrite the sentences and place the words in parentheses in the correct position.

1. *We arrived (last week, in Jamaica).*
    <u>*We arrived in Jamaica last week*</u>.

2. *It is (this morning, very windy).*

    _____ .

3. *You studied (yesterday, very hard).*

    _____ .

4. *He went (in a hurry, there).*

    _____ .

5. *She closed the door (carefully, very).*

_____ .

8. Find out the wrong alternative.

1. **a.** ☐ *I'm leaving home at 10.*
 b. ☑ *She is coming tomorrow home.*
 c. ☐ *She spoke quite loudly.*
 d. ☐ *You are quite right.*

2. **a.** ☐ *He here painted her picture.*
 b. ☐ *She often behaves generously.*
 c. ☐ *We are rarely late.*
 d. ☐ *The day was too hot.*

3. **a.** ☐ *They can never understand me.*
 b. ☐ *It rained during the night heavily.*
 c. ☐ *He waited outside nervously.*
 d. ☐ *We worked silently in the classroom yesterday.*

4. **a.** ☐ *I have almost finished.*
 b. ☐ *I saw your hat an hour ago somewhere.*
 c. ☐ *He had a great time last summer.*
 d. ☐ *We have too many buildings.*

5. **a.** ☐ *She has recently retired.*
 b. ☐ *He almost died.*
 c. ☐ *They walk in the evening quickly.*
 d. ☐ *We need more public transportation.*

Form of Adverbs

I write **slowly**.
He behaves **aggressively**.

BASICS

USING *-LY* (O USO DE *-LY*)

A maioria dos advérbios são formados acrescentando-se **-ly** a adjetivos.

sad – sad**ly**
(triste, tristemente)

beautiful – beautiful**ly**
(lindo, lindamente)

nice – nice**ly**
(bom, agradavelmente)

Também é possível transformar algumas palavras em adjetivos, através de afixos (prefixos e sufixos), e depois acrescentar **-ly**:

suffix	verb/noun	adjective	adverb
-able/-ably:	fashion (moda)	fashion**able** (moderno)	fashion**ably** (elegantemente)
-al/-ally:	magic (mágica)	magic**al** (mágico)	magic**ally** (magicamente)
-ate/-ately:	affection (afeição)	affection**ate** (afeiçoado)	affection**ately** (afeiçoadamente)
-ed/-edly:	worry (preocupar-se)	worri**ed** (preocupado)	worri**edly** (preocupadamente)
-ful/-fully:	peace (paz)	peace**ful** (pacífico)	peace**fully** (pacificamente)
-ial/-ially:	industry (indústria)	industr**ial** (industrial)	industr**ially** (industrialmente)
-ible/-ibly:	flex (flexionar)	flex**ible** (flexível)	flex**ibly** (flexivelmente)

-ic/-ically:	artist (artista)	artistic (artístico)	artistically (artisticamente)
-ical/-ically:	economy (economia)	economical (econômico)	economically (economicamente)
-ing/ingly:	annoy (importunar)	annoying (importuno)	annoyingly (importunadamente)
-ive/-ively:	attract (atrair)	attractive (atraente)	attractively (atraentemente)
-less/-lessly:	hope (esperança)	hopeless (desesperado)	hopelessly (desesperançadamente)
-ous/-ously:	glamour (glamour)	glamorous (glamouroso)	glamorously (glamourosamente)
-ular/-ularly:	spectacle (espetáculo)	spectacular (espetacular)	spectacularly (espetacularmente)

Notes:

* Adjetivos em **-ly** não formam advérbios. Nesses casos, são usadas formas substitutas:

*I am a **lonely** person.* > *I like living **in a lonely way**.*
(Sou uma pessoa solitária.) (Gosto de viver solitariamente.)

* Nem todas as palavras terminadas em **-ly** são advérbios.

* algumas são substantivos:
rally, folly
(rali, tolice)

* algumas são adjetivos:
holy, friendly, lovely, lonely, silly, elderly.
(santo, amigável, adorável, solitário, tolo, idoso)

*We organized a **rally** on the beach.*
(Organizamos um rally na praia.)

*We sent him a **friendly** letter.*

(Enviamos uma carta amigável a ele.)

*This is a **lovely** dining room*

(Esta sala de jantar é adorável.)

*She is a **lonely** woman.*

(Ela é uma mulher solitária.)

SPELLING (GRAFIA)

Ao acrescentar *-ly*, fique atento a possíveis mudanças na grafia.

✳ palavras em **-y** > mudam **y** para *i*.
   *hea**v**y – hea**vi**ly*   >   *la**z**y – la**zi**ly*
   (pesado/amente)   (preguiçoso/amente)

✳ palavras em **-able/-ible**, **-le** e algumas em **-e**, > perdem o **-e**.
   *tru**e** – tru**ly***   >   *simp**le** – simp**ly***
   (verdadeiro/amente)   (simples/mente)

✳ palavras em **-ic** > recebem **-ally**.
   *econom**ic** – economi**cally***   >   *trag**ic** – tragi**cally***
   (econômico/amente)   (trágico/amente)

COMPLEMENTARY

MULTIPLE FORMS (MÚLTIPLAS FORMAS)

Advérbios também podem ter...

✳ formação irregular:
   adj. – good (bom, bem)
   adv. – well (bem)

* ter a mesma forma que adjetivos:

close, deep, hard, fast, near, far, high, low, early, late, much etc.

(próximo, fundo, duro, rápido, perto, longe, alto, baixo, cedo, tarde, muito)

* ter duas formas com significados diferentes:

close - closely	*deep – deeply*	*hard – hardly*
(perto, atentamente)	(fundo, profundamente)	(duro, duramente)
high – highly	*late – lately*	*near – nearly*
(alto, altamente)	(tarde, ultimamente)	(perto, quase)

Observe:

Adjective	Adverb
*He is a **good** student.* (Ele é um bom aluno.) *I'm **well**, thank you.* (Estou bem, obrigado.)	*She speaks English **well**.* (Ela fala inglês bem.)
*He is a **close** friend of mine.* (Ele é meu amigo íntimo)	*Please, come **close**.* (Por favor, venha para perto.) *He watched the game **closely*** (Ele observou o jogo atentamente.)
*He is a **hard** worker.* (Ele é um trabalhador vigoroso.)	*He works **hard**.* (Ele trabalha pesado.) *I can **hardly** wait.* (Mal posso esperar.)
*I climb **high** mountains.* (Escalo altas montanhas.)	*The falcon flew **high** in the sky.* (O falcão voou alto no céu.) *She is a **highly** respected doctor.* (Ela é uma médica altamente respeitada.)
*A **late** student came in.* (Um aluno atrasado entrou.)	*I never get up **late**.* (Nunca levanto tarde.) *Have you seen him **lately**?* (Você o tem visto ultimamente?)

*It's a **near** distance.* (É uma curta distância.)	*I live **near** here.* (Moro perto daqui.) *I **nearly** fainted.* (Quase desmaiei.)
*That is a **deep** valley.* (Aquele é um vale profundo.)	*The house is **deep** in the woods.* (A casa fica escondida na floresta.) *He felt **deeply** sorry.* (Ele lamentou profundamente.)
*He is a **short** man.* (Ele é um homem baixo.)	*The car stopped **short**.* (O carro parou subitamente.) *We arrived **shortly** after 5.* (Chegamos logo depois das 5.)

Obs.: Também são advérbios os compostos por...

prep. + **subst.**: *aboard, ahead, away, besides, today etc.*
prep. + **adj.**: *abroad, along, aloud, around, behind, below etc.*
adv. + **prep.**: *hereafter, hereby, herein, thereupon etc.*
subst. + **wise**: *likewise, clockwise, crosswise etc.*
subst./adv. + **ward(s)**: *upward(s), eastward(s) etc.*

PRACTICE

(respostas na pág. 138)

1. Transform the adjectives into adverbs.

1. *gentle*   *gently*
2. *fair* _____
3. *loud* _____
4. *happy* _____
5. *basic* _____
6. *angry* _____
7. *terrible* _____
8. *boring* _____

9. *lucky* _____

10. *careful* _____

11. *probable* _____

12. *possible* _____

13. *rich* _____

14. *safe* _____

2. Underline the adverbs.

1. *He is <u>seriously</u> ill.*
2. *This book is really nice.*
3. *The story of "crazy man" was truly funny.*
4. *John drives very slowly.*
5. *He was talking too much angrily.*
6. *They live very happily.*
7. *He was driving carelessly.*
8. *John can speak French fluently.*
9. *They live happily.*
10. *We spend a week at that hotel annually.*

3. Complete the sentence using adverbs.

1. *The dog ran <u>quickly</u> . (quick)*
2. *She is always dressed _____ . (beautiful)*
3. *The results were _____ good. (relative)*
4. *Ann spoke about Grandpa _____ . (nice)*
5. *Joe spoke about his job _____ . (dramatic)*
6. *The teacher solved the problem _____ . (easy)*
7. *The children laughed _____ . (happy)*
8. *They are writing too _____ . (slow)*
9. *The people were _____ dressed. (poor)*
10. *My father drives very _____ . (careful)*

4. Choose the correct word.

1. *The crime occurred* _____ *before 3 a.m.*
   a. *short*   ***b.*** <u>*shortly*</u>

2. *John Lennon was a* _____ *great musician.*
   a. *truly*   ***b.*** *truely*

3. *Jean plays the piano* _____ .
   a. *goodly*   ***b.*** *well*

4. *It is* _____ *difficult to explain things to people.*
   a. *extremely*   ***b.*** *extremly*

5. *The chair is* _____ *made.*
   a. *bad*   ***b.*** *badly*

6. *My neighbor drives* _____ .
   a. *carelessly*   ***b.*** *carelly*

7. *The people were* _____ *disappointed by the election results.*
   a. *bitterly*   ***b.*** *bittery*

8. *You can* _____ *see famous actors in this district.*
   a. *frequent*   ***b.*** *frequently*

9. *Governments have to* _____ *care about the environment.*
   a. *seriously*   ***b.*** *serious*

10. *This is* _____ *the best restaurant in London.*
    a. *easily*   ***b.*** *easyly*

11. *11. Jennifer is laughing* _____ .
    a. *loud*   ***b.*** *loudly*

12. *He goes to school* _____ .
    a. *day*   *b.* *daily*

13. *The employees are paid* _____ .
    a. *monthly*   *b.* *month*

14. *He looked at me* _____ .
    a. *suspicious*   *b.* *suspiciously*

15. *He fought* _____ .
    a. *courageously*   *b.* *courageous*

5. Complete the sentences with words from the box.

> *badly   really   shortly   late   well   hardly*
> *early   lately   nearly   deeply*

1. *The course is ____nearly____ over.*
2. *I _____ don't believe him.*
3. *She could _____ walk after the show. She was too tired.*
4. *I got up _____ today. It was dark.*
5. *He will tell about his decision _____ after dinner.*
6. *She has been working hard _____ .*
7. *They're going to be _____ , for sure.*
8. *She is a good dancer. She dances really _____ .*
9. *He was _____ hurt.*
10. *I felt _____ sorry.*

6. Write down the correct adverb to complete the chart.

verb/noun	adjective	adverb
1. *rely*	*reliable*	*reliably*
2. *economy*	*economical*	_____

3.	*help*	*helpful*	_____
4.	*attention*	*attentive*	_____
5.	*disappoint*	*disappointing*	_____
6.	*charm*	*charming*	_____
7.	*breath*	*breathless*	_____
8.	*tire*	*tired*	_____

7. Match the synonyms.

a. *poorly*
b. *very much*
c. *incorrectly*
d. *cruelly*
e. *improperly*
f. *severely*

1. *This sofa is badly made.* (*a*)
2. *He speaks English badly.* ( )
3. *The teens behaved badly at the party.* ( )
4. *He treats his animals badly.* ( )
5. *I want that certificate badly.* ( )
6. *He was injured badly.* ( )

Adjective or Adverb?

He is a **kind** man.
He speaks **kindly**.

BASICS

Adjetivos são palavras que descrevem substantivos ou pronomes. Advérbios modificam verbos, adjetivos, outros advérbios ou mesmo frases inteiras, informando *onde, quando, como, porque* e *em que extensão* algo acontece.

ADJECTIVE (ADJETIVO)

* adjetivo modificando substantivo e pronome

*My <u>brother</u> is **kind**.*
(Meu irmão é carinhoso.)
*<u>Alice</u> is a **nice** girl.*
(Alice é uma garota atraente.)
*<u>She</u> is a **nice** girl.*
(Ela é uma garota atraente.)

ADVERB (ADVÉRBIO)

* advérbio modificando verbo

*He <u>talks</u> **kindly**.*
(Ele fala de maneira carinhosa.)

*I saw him **yesterday**.*

(Eu o vi ontem.)

*They came **here**.*

(Eles vieram aqui.)

✳ advérbio modificando adjetivo:

*She is **really** nice.*

(Ela é realmente atraente.)

*It is a **very** easy question.*

(É uma questão muito fácil.)

*I am **extremely** happy.*

(Estou extremamente feliz.)

✳ advérbio modificando outro advérbio

*You danced very **well**.*

(Você dançou muito bem.)

*Let's leave right **now**.*

(Vamos sair exatamente agora.)

*He played more **sadly** today.*

(Ele tocou de forma mais triste hoje.)

✳ advérbio modificando frase

***Unhappily**, the bus didn't stop.*

(Infelizmente, o ônibus não parou.)

***Certainly**, the weather is going to improve.*

(Certamente, o tempo vai melhorar.).

***Curiously**, we were wearing the same color.*

(Curiosamente, estávamos usando a mesma cor.)

LINKING VERBS[1] (VERBOS DE LIGAÇÃO)

Embora verbos de ligação como: *taste*, *smell*, *look*, *feel*, *grow*, *keep* etc. sejam na maioria das vezes seguidos por adjetivos, também podem ser acompanhados por advérbios. Os adjetivos informam sobre o sujeito. Os advérbios complementam o verbo.

* *look:*
  *The woman looked **angry**.*
  (A mulher parecia zangada.)
  *The woman looked **angrily** at us.*
  (A mulher nos olhou zangadamente.)

* *taste:*
  *This fish tastes **nice**.*
  (Este peixe tem gosto bom.)
  *Jerry tasted the food **carefully**.*
  (Jerry provou a comida cuidadosamente.)

* *smell:*
  *The dog smells **clean**.*
  (O cão tem cheiro de limpeza.)
  *The dog smelled the bone **slowly**.*
  (O cão cheirou o osso lentamente.)

* *feel:*
  *He felt **old**.*
  (Ele se sentiu velho.)
  *This fabric feels **lovely**.*
  (Este tecido é agradável ao toque.)

---

1. Linking verbs: become, appear, seem, look, smell, sound, taste, feel, grow, remain, prove, and stay.

PRACTICE

(respostas na pág. 140)

1. Underline the adjectives.

1. That was a _heavy_ rain, wasn't it?
2. The teacher was as clear as crystal.
3. A cat's urine glows under a black light.
4. The students' feedback was extremely positive.
5. She simply did a fantastic job with that song.
6. The general atmosphere at the meeting was great.
7. The grizzly bear is a large predator that is different from black bears.
8. The impala is a small African antelope.
9. The birth of gunpowder was accidental.
10. She's the calmest person I know.

2. Underline the adverbs.

1. She _never_ smokes.
2. He lives exceedingly far.
3. Jeremy goes to school daily.
4. He ran fast to catch the bus.
5. I will always remember them.
6. Barking dogs seldom bite.
7. The cheetah ran incredibly quickly.
8. That is a very old brick house.
9. She jumped amazingly high.
10. She spoke extremely confidently.

3. Classify the underlined words as **Adj.** (adjective) or **Adv.** (adverb).

	Adj.	Adv.
1. My sister grew _angry_.	✓	
2. The plant grew _quickly_.		

3. *The students look <u>cheerful</u>.* _____ _____
4. *My brother looked <u>cheerfully</u> at the cake.* _____ _____
5. *They left <u>unusually</u> early.* _____ _____
6. *They left a <u>white</u> dog here.* _____ _____
7. *I love <u>fast</u> cars.* _____ _____
8. *My friend drives <u>fast</u>.* _____ _____
9. *John arrived <u>late</u>.* _____ _____
10. *I'm watching the <u>late</u> film.* _____ _____
11. *Sarah <u>quickly</u> ate her lunch.* _____ _____
12. *She had time for a <u>quick</u> meal.* _____ _____
13. *This magazine is published <u>weekly</u>.* _____ _____
14. *This is a <u>weekly</u> magazine.* _____ _____
15. *The coach spoke <u>confidently</u> to the boys.* _____ _____

4. Choose the correct alternatives to complete the sentences.

1. *Ann is quite (timid/timidly) _____<u>timid</u>_____ and speaks (soft/softly) _____<u>softly</u>_____ .*
2. *This problem is (harder/hardly) _____ than I thought.*
3. *He is (possible/possibly) _____ going to win the election.*
4. *The Olympic Games are held (quadrennial/quadrennially) _____ _____ .*
5. *He walked to the park (slow/slowly) _____ .*
6. *We grew (tired/tiredly) _____ working on Sundays.*
7. *The exam was (extreme/extremely) _____ difficult.*
8. *Liverpool is a lively, (modern/modernly) _____ city.*
9. *She knows the Italian culture very (good/well) _____ .*
10. *The birds were flying (surprising/surprisingly) _____ low.*
11. *The children were (complete/completely) _____ lost.*
12. *We will most (certain/certainly) _____ meet her.*
13. *The skies became surprisingly (dark/darkly) _____ .*
14. *They (quick/quickly) _____ rebuilt the city after the war.*
15. *(Unfortunate/Unfortunately) _____ , I didn't talk to him.*

5. Complete the sentences with words from the box.

> tragically   simply   sadly   nicely   wholly   lazily
> truly   heavily   furiously   quickly

1. *He is sad. He sings _____sadly_____ .*
2. *She dresses _____ . She is a very elegant lady.*
3. *We walked _____ through the snow.*
4. *It was hot and the cat walked _____ on the roof top.*
5. *He is _____ a good friend.*
6. *She believes that life is _____ good.*
7. *It is _____ a matter of time.*
8. *He died _____ in a car accident.*
9. *She was very angry and left the room _____ .*
10. *He felt sick and drove _____ to the hospital.*

Comparison of Adjectives and Adverbs

The **most beautiful** girl in town.
The most **beautifully** designed temple.

BASICS

Tanto adjetivos como advérbios podem ser usados nos graus normal, comparativo e superlativo (*positive, comparative and superlative degrees*).

positive	comparative	superlative
beautiful	*more beautiful*	*most beautiful*
beautifully	*more beautifully*	*most beautifully*

O grau **comparativo** é usado para comparar dois itens; o grau **superlativo** é usado para comparar um item com o resto do grupo ao qual ele pertence.

*The white house is **taller** than the blue one.*
(A casa branca é mais alta que a azul.)
*It is the **taller** of the two houses.*
(É a mais alta das duas casas.)
*It is the **tallest** house in town.*
(É a casa mais alta da cidade.)
*This is the **most beautifully** designed restaurant I know.*
(Este é o restaurante com o design mais bonito que conheço.)

A forma do adjetivo ou advérbio vai depender do número de sílabas. Palavras com uma ou duas silabas são consideradas "curtas". Palavras com duas ou mais sílabas são consideradas "longas".

FORM (FORMA)

* *more/most* + **palavras "longas"**

positive	comparative	superlative
difficult (difícil; adj.)	*more difficult*	*most difficult*
quickly (rapidamente; adv.)	*more quickly*	*most quickly*
easily (facilmente; adv.)	*more easily*	*most easily*

*English is **more difficult** than geography.*

(Inglês é mais difícil do que Geografia.)

*I think math is the **most difficult** of the three.*

(Eu acho Matemática a mais difícil das três.)

Obs.: adjetivos terminados em *-ful*, *-ous*, *-re*, *-ing*, *-ed* e muitos advérbios terminados em *-ly* seguem a mesma regra.

joy**ful**	fam**ous**	obscu**re**	amaz**ing**	skill**ed**	slow**ly**
(feliz)	(famoso)	(obscuro)	(surpreso)	(habilidoso)	(lentamente)

*He has the **most obscure** function I've heard of.*

(Ele tem a função mais obscura sobre a qual já ouvi falar.)

*Grandpa drives **more slowly** than Grandma.*

(Vovô dirige mais lentamente do que vovó.)

He is More Famous tha You *is a comedy film.*

(*Ele é Mais Famoso do que Você* é um filme de comédia.)

* **palavras "curtas" + *er/est***

positive	comparative	superlative
new (adj. novo)	*newer*	*newest*
small (adj. pequeno)	*smaller*	*smallest*
late (adv. tarde)	*later*	*latest*
early (adv. cedo)	*earlier*	*earliest*

*He arrived **earlier** than you.*
(Ele chegou mais cedo do que você.)
*These are the **smallest** sculptures I've made.*
(Estas são as menores esculturas que fiz.)

Obs.: adjetivos de 2 sílabas terminados em **-er**, **-y**, **-ow** seguem a mesma regra:

clever[1]	***pretty***	***narrow***
(esperto)	(bonito)	(estreito)

*He is the **cleverest** student in his group.*
(Ele é o aluno mais esperto de seu grupo.)
*She is **prettier** than her sister.*
(Ela é mais bonita do que sua irmã.)
*This is the **narrowest** street in town.*
(Esta é a rua mais estreita da cidade.)

SPELLING (GRAFIA)

Ao acrescentar **-er/-est**, fique atento às mudanças na grafia das palavras.

---

1. As palavras **clever, gentle, friendly, quiet, simple** podem seguir qualquer das duas regras: **cleverer/more clever; friendlier/most friendly; simpler/more simple** etc.

✳ palavra terminada em **-y** > muda **y** para **i**.

happy (feliz)	*happier*	*happiest*
angry (zangado)	*angrier*	*angriest*

✳ palavra terminada em **-e** > recebe apenas **-r/-st**.

large (amplo)	*larger*	*largest*
wise (sábio)	*wiser*	*wisest*

✳ palavra terminada em consoante/vogal/consoante > *dobra* a consoante:

hot (quente)	*hotter*	*hottest*
thin (magro)	*thinner*	*thinnest*

I'm happier today than yesterday.
(Estou mais feliz hoje do que ontem.)
That was the largest street in town.
(Aquela era a maior rua da cidade.)
This is the hottest month of the year.
(Este é o mês mais quente do ano.)

COMPLEMENTARY

IRREGULAR COMPARISON (COMPARAÇÃO IRREGULAR)

Alguns adjetivos e advérbios formam os graus comparativo e superlativo de maneira irregular.

adj./adv.	comparative	superlative
good, well (bom, bem)	*better*	*best*
bad, badly (mau, mal)	*worse*	*worst*

little (pouco)	*less*	*least*
much, many (muito/s)	*more*	*most*
far (longe)	*farther, further*[2]	*farthest, furthest*

*Karl is a **good** teacher but James is **better** than Karl.*

(Karl é um bom professor, mas James é melhor do que Paul.)

*You sing **well** but I sing **better** than you.*

(Você canta bem, mas eu canto melhor do que você.)

*My sister is the **worst** person I know.*

(Minha irmã é a pior pessoa que conheço.)

*The silk scarf costs **little** but the cotton one costs **less**.*

(O cachecol de seda custa pouco, mas o de algodão custa menos.)

*This street has **less** traffic than that street.*

(Esta rua tem menos tráfico que aquela.)

*You say you gave me **much** love, but he gave me **more** love than you.*

(Você diz que me deu muito amor, mas ele me deu mais amor do que você.)

*Do you live **farther** than Meg?*

(Você mora mais longe do que a Meg?)

*Give me **further** details, please.*

(Dê-me mais detalhes, por favor.)

Obs.: Adjetivos compostos sofrem mudanças apenas na primeira parte da palavra.

***good**-smelling* (cheiroso)	***better**-smelling*	***best**-smelling*
***well**-known* (notório)	***better**-known*	***best**-known*

CONSTRUCTIONS WITH COMPARISONS
(CONSTRUÇÕES COM COMPARAÇÕES)

Adjetivos e advérbios são usados em construções que expressam comparação.

2. Farther/farthest – distance; further/furthest – extent.

✴ *as ... as, not so ... as* (tão ... quanto, não tão ... quanto)

Esta construção é usada com as palavras no grau normal.

*Stay **as** long **as** you wish.*
(Fique tanto quanto desejar.)
*She is not **as/so** bright **as** her sister.*
(Ela não é tão brilhante quanto a irmã.)

✴ *the (comparative) ... the (comparative)* (quanto mais ... melhor)

Esta construção expressa crescimento paralelo *(parallel increase)*. É usada com as palavras no grau comparativo.

The sooner** we get there, **the better.
(Quanto mais cedo chegarmos, melhor.)
***The more** you complain, **the worse** it gets.*
(Quanto mais você reclamar, pior fica.)
***The more difficult** the struggle, **the more glorious** the thiumph.*
(Quanto mais difícil a batalha, mais glorioso o triunfo.)

✴ *(comparative) and (comparative)* (mais e mais ...)

Esta construção expressa crescimento gradual *(gradual increase/ double comparative)*. É usada com as palavras no grau comparativo.

*The day is getting **colder and colder**.*
(O dia está cada vez mais frio.)
*He is getting **more and more interested**.*
(Ele está cada vez mais interessado.)
*Things are getting **worse and worse**.*
(As coisas estão cada vez piores.)

PRACTICE

(respostas na pág. 140)

1. Write the comparative and superlative forms of these adjectives.

1.	*thin*	*thinner*	*thinnest*
2.	*big*		
3.	*good*		
4.	*old*		
5.	*expensive*		
6.	*short*		
7.	*late*		
8.	*heavy*		
9.	*interesting*		
10.	*bad*		

2. Write the comparative and superlative forms of these adverbs.

1.	*near*	*nearer*	*nearest*
2.	*proudly*		
3.	*quickly*		
4.	*dangerously*		
5.	*well*		
6.	*badly*		
7.	*heavily*		
8.	*sadly*		
9.	*slowly*		
10.	*fast*		

3. Complete the sentences with the comparative form of the words in parentheses.

1. (*good*) *In a lab experiment chimps performed* __better__ *than humans on a number memory test.*

2. (long) A rat can last _____ without water than a camel.
3. (big) An ostrich's eye is _____ than its brain.
4. (weak) The tarantula is actually harmless to humans with a venom _____ than that of a bee's sting.
5. (fast) A rhino can run _____ than 35 mph.
6. (many) Hippos have killed _____ people in Africa than any other wild animal.
7. (smart) Dolphins are known to be _____ than almost any other creature on earth.
8. (many) Cats have _____ vocal sounds – one hundred – than dogs – about ten.
9. (fast) Dragonflies fly _____ than bees.
10. (large) The tiger is a _____ cat than the lion.
11. (small/agile) Female lions are _____ and _____ than males.
12. (much) A bird requires _____ food in proportion to its size than a baby or a cat.
13. (attractive) Males of some animal species are _____ than females.
14. (little) The bones of a pigeon weigh _____ than its feathers.
15. (aggressive) A male hippopotamus exhibits _____ behavior than the female hippo.

4. Complete the sentences with the superlative form of the words in parentheses.

1. (lazy) Lions are the _____laziest_____ of the big cats; they spend 16-20 hours of the day resting or sleeping.
2. (intelligent) The chimpanzee is considered the _____ primate.
3. (good) An elephant has one of the _____ memories in the animal kingdom.
4. (common) The mouse is the _____ mammal in the US.
5. (fast) The _____ bird on land is the ostrich, which runs at 69 km per hour (43 miles per hour).

6. *(smart/clean) Pigs are perhaps the* _____ , _____ *domestic animals known.*

7. *(brainy) Cephalopods are certainly among the* _____ *invertebrates in the sea.*

8. *(fast) The cheetah is the* _____ *land animal – it achieves between 112 and 120 km/h, and has the ability to accelerate from 0 to over 100 km/h in three seconds.*

9. *(large) The world's* _____ *spider had a leg-span of 28 cm. It was found in the coastal rainforests of Surinam, Guyana and French Guiana.*

10. *(loud) The blue whale is the* _____ *animal on earth. Their sounds can travel for many miles underwater.*

11. *(acute) The* _____ *sense of smell are male emperor moths. They can detect a female from almost 11 km away.*

12. *(deep) Leatherback turtles take the* _____ *dive made by a reptile. They can reach depths of 1,200m.*

13. *(long) Humpback whales travel the* _____ *distances – more than 16,000km every year on the round trip from Antarctica to Costa Rica.*

14. *(short/long) The American opossum has the* _____ *gestation period – 12 to 13 days. The* _____ *is the Asiatic elephant, taking 608 days.*

15. *(large/small) The* _____ *egg from a living bird belongs to the ostrich and the* _____ *bird egg is produced by the hummingbird.*

5. Circle the correct alternative.

1. *The* _____ *muscle in the body is the* tongue.
   a. <u>strongest</u>   *b.* stronger

2. *Papyrus was used* _____ *than paper.*
   a. earliest   *b.* earlier

3. *Dad is the* _____ *person I know.*
   a. more serious   **b.** most serious

4. *She greeted me* _____ *of all.*
   a. more politely   **b.** the most politely

5. *I speak English* _____ *today than last year.*
   a. more fluently   **b.** fluentliest

6. *The Sartorius muscle is the* _____ *muscle in the human body.*
   a. longest   **b.** longer

7. *Candice is the* _____ *singer who's ever been on a TV show.*
   a. more gifted   **b.** most gifted

8. *This girl dances the* _____ *of all.*
   a. most gracefully   **b.** more gracefully

9. *He works a lot* _____ *carefully than the other dentist in town.*
   a. less   **b.** least

10. *DDT was the* _____ *pesticide in the world.*
    a. more widely-used   **b.** most widely-used

11. *Of the two brothers, he is by far the* _____ .
    a. faster   **b.** fastest

12. *She is wearing her* _____ *dress for the meeting.*
    a. finer   **b.** finest

6. Complete the sentences with expressions from the box.

> *the better   the less   the sooner*
> *the more difficult   the higher   the cheaper*

1. *The quicker you finish this project,* ___*the better*___ *.*
2. *The bigger the demand is,* _____ *prices you get.*
3. *The more you sell,* _____ *you can sell.*
4. *The more you think about it,* _____ *the problem seems to be.*
5. *The faster we do it,* _____ *we'll leave.*
6. *The more we saw,* _____ *we could believe.*

7. Match the sentence parts.

a. *more and more difficult.*
b. *more and more expensive.*
c. *higher and higher*
d. *less and less.*
e. *is better and better.*
f. *It is more and more boring*

1. *The problem is getting more and more difficult.* (*a*)
2. _____ *to find a parking place.* ( )
3. *Food is* _____ *.* ( )
4. *Australian wine* _____ *.* ( )
5. *Prices are getting* _____ *over the years.* ( )
6. *She is eating* _____ *.* ( )

8. Choose the correct word to complete the expressions.

> *busy   flat   quiet   red   cold   hungry   big   white*
> *soon   old   innocent   free   clear   easy   sick*

1. *I was as <u>busy</u> as a bee over the weekend.*
2. *My grandpa is very old. He's as* _____ *as the hills.*
3. *Kansas is as* _____ *as a pancake.*
4. *Please, send me it as* _____ *as possible.*
5. *He didn't make a sound. He was as* _____ *as a mouse.*

6. She went as _____ as a ghost when she saw me.
7. She is very shy. Her face went as _____ as a beetroot.
8. He came into the room and stood there as _____ as life.
9. Don't go outside. It is as _____ as ice.
10. When he arrived he was as _____ as a bear.
11. I was as _____ as crystal about my intentions.
12. This game is as _____ as pie.
13. I feel as _____ as a bird when I go to the beach.
14. I have to go home. I feel as _____ as a dog.
15. She didn't do that. She is as _____ as a lamb.

Common Mistakes

He is my **only** brother.
I invited **only** my brother.

COMPLEMENTARY

Dentre os problemas mais comuns no uso de adjetivos e advérbios estão os causados por:

* erro de posicionamento;
* erro de significado;
* erro de diferenciação entre adjetivo e advérbio.

Observe os casos a seguir.

ONLY (único; apenas, somente, simplesmente, só)

* adjetivo > antes de substantivos.
  *I was an **only** child.*
  (Fui filho único.)
  *That was the **only** pencil I had.*
  (Era o único lápis que eu tinha.)

* advérbio > junto à palavra que modifica; no fim da frase (mais genérico).
  She hurt him on the nose.
  ***Only** she hurt him on the nose.*
  (Apenas ela o feriu no nariz.)
  *She **only** hurt him on the nose.*
  (Ela apenas o feriu no nariz.)
  *She hurt **only** him on the nose.*
  (Ela feriu apenas a ele no nariz.)

*She hurt him **only** on the nose.*

(Ela o feriu apenas no nariz.)

*She hurt him on the nose **only**.*

(Ela o feriu no nariz apenas.)

ENOUGH (bastante, suficiente; suficientemente)

* adjetivo > antes de substantivos.

*I have **enough** money.*

(Tenho dinheiro suficiente.)

*Do we have **enough** time?*

(Temos tempo suficiente?)

* advérbio > após adjetivos, advérbios e verbos.

*These shoes are not big **enough**.*

(Esses sapatos não são suficientemente grandes.)

*He is strong **enough** to help us.*

(Ele é forte suficiente para nos ajudar.)

*I arrived soon **enough**.*

(Cheguei cedo o suficiente.)

*I work quickly **enough**.*

(Trabalho suficientemente rápido.)

*She didn't run fast **enough** to catch the bus.*

(Ela não correu rápido o suficiente para pegar o ônibus.)

TOO (demais, também)

* advérbio > antes de adjetivos e advérbios.

*She ran **too** fast.*

(Ela correu demasiadamente rápido.)

*He works **too** quickly.*

(Ele trabalha rápido demais.)

*They talk **too** much.*

(Eles falam demais.)

*This car is **too** old for me to buy.*

(Este carro é velho demais para eu comprar.)

*He is **too** young to drive.*

(Ele é jovem demais para dirigir.)

Obs.: Quando no final da frase *(= também)*, deve ser precedido por vírgula.

*I like ice cream and coffee, **too**.*

(Gosto de sorvete e de café também.)

VERY (exato, simples, muito)

* adjetivo > antes de substantivos.
  *It was that **very** day that he proposed to her.*

  (Foi naquele mesmo dia que ele propôs a ela.)

  *The **very** mention of the event makes me cry.*

  (A simples menção do acontecimento me faz chorar.)

* advérbio > antes de adjetivos.
  *This method is **very** efficient.*

  (Este método é muito eficiente.)

  *The film was **very** interesting.*

  (O filme foi muito interessante.)

  *He was **very** bored.*

  (Ele estava muito entediado.)

FAIRLY, RATHER (bem, razoavelmente, um tanto quanto)

Os dois advérbios têm significados próximos mas não idênticos.

✳ *fairly* > geralmente expressa aprovação.
*This box is **fairly** light.*

(Esta caixa é leve.)

*This coffee is **fairly** strong.*

(O café está razoavelmente forte.)

*That is a **fairly** interesting book.*

(É um livro bem interessante.)

✳ *rather* > geralmente expressa desaprovação; também usado em comparações.
*This coffee is **rather** strong.*

(O café está um tanto quanto forte.)

*That is a **rather** bad book.*

(É um livro bem ruim.)

*The room was **rather** worse than I had expected.*

(O quarto era um tanto quanto pior do que eu esperava.)

*Jill is **fairly** clever but her brother is **rather** stupid.*

(Jill é bem inteligente mas o irmão dela é bem obtuso.)

> mas, com palavras positivas, *rather* é mais enfático que *fairly* *(= very)*

*She is **rather** pretty.*

(Ela é bastante bonita.)

*This is **rather** good.*

(Isto é bastante bom.)

*He is **rather** intelligent.*

(Ele é bem inteligente.)

GOOD, WELL (bom; bem)

✳ *good* (adj) > antes de substantivos; após verbos de ligação.
*You did a **good** job.*

(Você fez um bom trabalho.)

*I feel **good**.*

(Sinto-me bem. = estado)

*It **smells** good.*

(Cheira bem.)

*You look **good** in blue.*

(Você fica bem de azul.)

*The weather **looks** good today.*

(O tempo parece bom hoje.)

* ***well*** (adj.) > referindo-se a saúde
*I feel **well** today.*

(Sinto-me bem hoje.)

*You did not look **well** yesterday.*

(Você não parecia bem ontem.)

* ***well*** (adv.) > indicando modo
*You did the job **well**.*

(Você fez bem o trabalho.)

*You cook **well**.*

(Você cozinha bem.)

*It was a **well** organized plan.*

(Foi um plano bem organizado.)

*She plays **well** enough to win.*

(Ela joga bem o suficiente para vencer.)

The dog smelled the cat well.

(O cão cheirou bem o gato.)

BAD, BADLY (mau, ruim, desfavorável; mal, muito, seriamente, gravemente)

* ***bad*** (adj.)
*I feel **bad**.*

(Eu estou/me sinto mal. = saúde/emoção)

*I am **bad**.*

(Não estou bem = saúde.)

*This dog smells **bad**.*

(Este cão cheira mal.)

*She was in a **bad** mood.*

(Ela estava de mau humor.)

*I had a **bad** night.*

(Tive uma noite ruim.)

*You made a **bad** impression.*

(Você deu uma má impressão.)

✳ badly (adv.)

*You play football **badly**.*

(Você joga futebol mal.)

*He performed **badly**.*

(Ele atuou mal.)

*It doesn't hurt so **badly** now.*

(Não dói muito agora.)

*He needs help **badly**.*

(Ele precisa seriamente de ajuda.)

*He cut himself **badly**.*

(Ele se cortou seriamente.)

*He was **badly** hurt.*

(Ele ficou gravemente ferido.)

*A **badly** written letter.*

(Uma carta mau escrita.)

*My old dog smells **badly**.*

(Meu velho cão está ruim de faro.)

SURE, SURELY (certo; certamente, de fato)

✳ sure (adj)

*I am **sure** that he was there.*

(Tenho certeza que ele estava lá.)

*He is **sure** to be a great leader.*

(Ele está certo de ser um grande líder.)

*Are you **sure**?*

(Tem certeza?)

✳ surely (adv.)

*He is **surely** ready to leave.*

(Ele, de fato, está pronto para sair.)

*You **surely** wanted to go there.*

(Você certamente queria ir lá.)

*It was **surely** inevitable.*

(Foi certamente inevitável.)

***Surely**, you can see that.*

(Certamente, você consegue ver isso.)

REAL, REALLY (real, genuíno; realmente)

✳ real (adj.)

*That actor has **real** charm.*

(Aquele ator tem um encanto genuíno.)

*The film is based on **real** life.*

(O filme é baseado na vida real.)

*Who is the **real** boss?*

(Quem é o verdadeiro chefe?)

✳ really (adv.)

*She is **really** charismatic.*

(Ela é realmente carismática.)

*He is **really** very clever.*

(Ele é realmente muito inteligente.)

*That was a **really** enjoyable day.*

(Foi um dia realmente agradável.)

***Really**, you should have told me.*

(Realmente, você deveria ter me dito.)

NEAR, NEARLY (perto, próximo; quase, aproximadamente)

* **near** (adj.)
  *It will be in the **near** future.*
  (Será num futuro próximo.)
  *She was **near** tears.*
  (Ela estava quase em lágrimas.)
  *He is a **near** relative.*
  (Ele é um parente próximo.)
  *She is a **near** friend.*
  (Ela é uma amiga chegada.)

* **near** (adv.)
  *He was **near** killed.*
  (Ele quase foi morto.)
  *Do you live **near** here?*
  (Você mora perto daqui?)
  *Stay **near** the door.*
  (Fique perto da porta.)
  *He lives quite **near**.*
  (Ele mora bem perto.)

* **nearly** (adv.)
  *We created **nearly** 700 jobs.*
  (Criamos quase 700 empregos.)
  *The coat **nearly** fits.*
  (O casaco quase serve.)
  *I **nearly** died with cold.*
  (Quase morri de frio.)
  *The beach was **nearly** empty.*
  (A praia estava quase vazia.)

SHORT, SHORTLY (curto, breve; subitamente, logo, brevemente, rudemente)

✳ *short* (adj.)
*We had a **short** holiday.*
(Tivemos umas férias curtas.)
*We had a **short** talk today.*
(Tivemos uma breve conversa hoje.)
*He wrote two **short** stories.*
(Ele escreveu dois contos.)
*Be **short** and to the point.*
(Seja breve e direto.)

✳ *short* (adv.)
*He stopped **short**.*
(Ele parou abruptamente.)

✳ *shortly* (adv.)
*You will hear from us **shortly**.*
(Você vai saber de nós em breve.)
*He arrived **shortly** before me.*
(Ele chegou pouco antes de mim.)
*They will come **shortly**.*
(Eles chegarão logo.)

SLOW, SLOWLY (lento, devagar; lentamente)

✳ *slow* (adj.)
*He is a **slow** worker.*
(Ele é um trabalhador lento.)
*The service here is very **slow**.*
(O serviço aqui é lento.)
*That watch is 10 minutes **slow**.*
(Esse relógio está 10 minutos atrasado.)

109

* **slowly** (adv.)
  *He speaks **slowly**.*
  (Ele fala lentamente.)
  *She walks **slowly**.*
  (Ela anda devagar.)

BARELY, SCARCELY, HARDLY (apenas, mal, quase não, quase nunca, raramente).

Os três advérbios têm significado negativo muito próximo. Não devem ser usados com verbos na forma negativa.

*I had **barely/scarcely/hardly** sat down at the table, when he arrived.*
(Eu mal havia sentado à mesa quando ele chegou.)

* **barely**
  *He could **barely** see him.*
  (Eu mal pude vê-lo.)
  *She has **barely** enough to eat.*
  (Ela quase não tem o que comer.)
  *He is **barely** sixteen.*
  (Ele não tem mais de dezesseis anos.)
  *He **barely** escaped death.*
  (Ele quase não escapou da morte.)

* **scarcely**
  *We can **scarcely** see the way.*
  (Mal conseguimos ver o caminho.)
  *I can **scarcely** believe it.*
  (Mal posso acreditar.)
  *There was **scarcely** a tree left.*
  (Não sobrou quase nenhuma árvore.)

* *hardly* > mais usado com *can*, *ever*, *any*

*I could **hardly** breath.*

(Eu mal podia respirar.)

*I have **hardly** any money.*

(Quase não tenho nenhum dinheiro.)

***Hardly** anyone came to the party.*

(Quase ninguém foi à festa.)

ALREADY, STILL, YET (já; ainda, já, entretanto, até agora)

Usa-se *already* quando algo já aconteceu; *still* quando algo está acontecendo e *yet* quando algo ainda não aconteceu.

* *already* > Expressa surpresa sobre o acontecido.

meio/fim da frase:
*I've **already** finished my report.*

(Já terminei meu relatório.)

*I've finished my report **already**.*

(Já terminei meu relatório.)

*Have you **already** finished your report?*

(Você já terminou seu relatório?)

* *still* > denota algo acontecendo.

antes do verbo principal:
*I am **still** writing my report.*

(Ainda estou fazendo meu relatório.)

após verbo to be:
*He is **still** at home.*

(Ele ainda está em casa.)

após o suj. (neg./int.):
*I **still** don't understand it.*

(Ainda não entendo.)

*Are you **still** here?*

(Você ainda está aqui?)

* **yet** > expressa expectativa sobre algo que não aconteceu.

fim da frase (neg./int.):
*I haven't finished my report **yet**.*

(Ainda não terminei meu relatório.)

*Aren't you ready **yet**?*

(Você ainda não está pronto?)

INVERSION (INVERSÃO)

Inversões são geralmente usadas na linguagem escrita para enfatizar algo que vai ser dito.

Quando iniciando a frase houver palavras como **up**, **down**, **in**, **out**, **back** etc. ou palavras de sentido negativo como **never**, **hardly**, **not only**, **no sooner** etc. > coloca-se o verbo antes do sujeito.

***Under** the road run water pipes.*

(Canos de água passam sob a estrada.)

***Here** is the bridge.*

(Aqui está a ponte.)

***Out** went the light.*

(Acabou a luz.)

***Never** has he arrived late.*

(Ele nunca chegou tarde.)

***Seldom** has a person had so many chances.*

(Raramente alguém teve tantas oportunidades.)

***Never** would I be persuaded to follow them.*

(Eu nunca seria persuadido a segui-los.)

__Not__ in a thousand years would I invite her.

(Eu não a convidaria nem em mil anos.)

Alguns verbos usam o auxiliar *__do__* para a inversão.

__Rarely__ do you find such honest people.

(Raramente encontramos pessoas tão honestas.)

__No sooner__ did we hear the results than he arrived.

(Assim que ouvimos/Mal ouvimos os resultados quando ele chegou.)

Obs: a inversão não é necessária quando o sujeito é um pronome.

__Here__ he is.

(Aqui está ele.)

__There__ you are.

(Aí está você.)

LISTING (ENUMERAÇÃO)

Evite enumerar mais do que três ou quatro itens de cada vez. Dê preferência a números ordinais e não a advérbios em *-ly* como: *__first-ly__*[1], *__secondly__* etc.

__First__, he is quite unclear. __Second__, it's a bad decision.

(Primeiro, ele não é claro. Segundo, é uma decisão ruim.)

PRACTICE

(respostas na pág. 142)

1. Check the sentence containing *__only__* as adjective.

1. *She only talks to her brother.* ☐
2. *Only she talks to her brother.* ☐

1. **First** pode ser adjetivo ou advérbio.

(adj.) The **first** man on the planet. (adv.) Phone **first** if you are dropping by.

Deve, preferencialmente, ser usado em lugar de **firstly**.

3. She talks to her only brother. ☐
4. Only during World War II, a bomb killed an elephant in the Berlin Zoo. ☐
5. A bomb dropped on Berlin killed the only elephant in the Berlin Zoo. ☐
6. Only a bomb dropped on Berlin killed the elephant in the Berlin Zoo. ☐
7. A bomb dropped on Berlin killed the elephant in the Berlin Zoo only. ☐

2. Match sentence to meaning.

1. Only the man ate the soup for dinner. ( )
2. The man only ate the soup for dinner. ( )
3. The man ate the soup for dinner only. ( )
4. The man ate only the soup for dinner. ( )

a. Soup was the only food he ate.
b. No one but the man ate the soup.
c. The man merely ate the soup; he didn't drop it.
d. The man ate something different for breakfast and lunch.

3. Complete the sentences using *enough*. Then check **Adj.** *(for adjective)* or **Adv.** *(for adverb)*.

1. There are not ____enough____ chairs for all of us. <u>Adj.</u>
2. She is old _____ to ride a horse. _____
3. He spoke slowly _____ for me to understand. _____
4. If you study hard _____ you will pass the test. _____
5. I don't get _____ support from my coach. _____
6. The soup isn't hot _____ . _____
7. Are there _____ sandwiches for all of the kids? _____

4. Underline the correct alternative.

1. *You drive so slow/<u>slowly</u> that I'm going on foot.*
2. *He knows the material very good/well.*
3. *That shop sells good/well furniture.*
4. *That car is too/very expensive. I can't afford it.*
5. *He is a bad/badly guy and manages that company bad/badly.*
6. *Are you sure/surely this is the correct road?*
7. *This dress is too/very short. It won't fit me.*
8. *The apple pie smells good/well.*
9. *They were arrested short/shortly after arriving in NY.*
10. *He sings my favorite song good/well.*
11. *The ice cream tasted good/well last night.*
12. *I works good/well with many people.*
13. *My house is too/very small but we love it.*
14. *We were talking and near/nearly missed the bus.*
15. *Wild turkeys can fly for short/shortly distances at up to 55 miles per hour.*

5. Complete the sentences. Use *fairly* or *rather*.

1. *I hope the exercise will be _____fairly_____ easy.*
2. *Well, I think the task will be _____ difficult.*
3. *The kitchen looks _____ clean.*
4. *The chicken was _____ badly cooked.*
5. *Your hands look _____ dirty.*
6. *We live _____ near. We love it.*
7. *He lives _____ far. He intends to move closer.*
8. *This room looks _____ tiny for eight people.*
9. *By the end of the day we were _____ tired.*
10. *The lecture was _____ interesting.*

6. Complete the sentences. Use *yet*, *still* or *already*.

1. *Have you found a solution to this problem _____yet/already_____ ?*

2. *Are you* _____ *working for the same company?*
3. *He hasn't sent the results* _____ .
4. *Is John* _____ *here? I thought he had* _____
   gone home.
5. *Is John* _____ *here? He was supposed to come only in*
   the afternoon.
6. *The lecture had* _____ *started when we arrived.*
7. *Are you* _____ *in the same job?*
8. *Are you in the new job* _____ *?*
9. *Are you in the same job* _____ *?*
10. *I am* _____ *in the same job.*

7. Rewrite the sentences. Use inversion.

1. *She had never done that before.*
   Never had she done that before.

2. *Joseph is seldom late.*

   _____ .

3. *The dog could be found nowhere.*

   _____ .

4. *I had almost finished the chapter when he arrived.*

   _____ .

5. *I can accept cheques under no circumstances.*

   _____ .

6. *A bunch of flowers was on the doorstep.*

   _____ .

7. *I have never felt so calm.*

   _____ .

Appendix

MOST COMMON ADJECTIVES *(descriptive and quantitative)*[1]

A

abrupt	agreeable	annoyed
absorbent	alert	annoying
abundant	alive	anxious
abusive	**all**	**any**
accessible	amazing	artistic
accidental	ambiguous	arrogant
active	ambitious	ashamed
adaptable	amused	atomic
adorable	amusing	attractive
adventurous	ancient	average
afraid	angry	awful

B

babyish	black	breezy
bad	blue	brief
bad-tempered	blue-eyed	bright
bearded	bluish	British
beautiful	boiling	broad
better	bored	broken
bewildered	boring	brown
big	brave	brownish
bitter	Brazilian	businesslike

C

calm	careless	cheerful
capable	charming	childish
careful	chemical	childlike

1. Em negrito: quantitative adjectives.

chilly
Chinese
chubby
clean
clever
cloudy
clumsy
coherent
cold
cold-blooded
colorful

colorless
colossal
comfortable
conditional
confident
confused
convertible
cool
cooperative
costly

courageous
crazy
creative
credible
creepy
crooked
cruel
curly
curved
cynical

D

daily
damaged
damp
dangerous
dark-haired
dazzling
dead
deadly
deceitful
decisive
deductive
deep
defeated
defiant
delicious

delightful
democratic
departmental
dependent
depressed
desirous
determined
different
diligent
dirty
disagreeable
disappointed
disconnected
discreet

diseased
disgusted
disgusting
dishonest
disorganized
disturbed
dizzy
doubtful
down-to-earth
drinkable
dry
dull
dusty
dynamic

E

eager
early
easy
easy-going
eatable
educational

effective
efficient
elated
elegant
embarrassed
eminent

empty
enchanting
encouraging
endurable
energetic
English

enjoyable
enough
entertaining
enthusiastic

envious
erratic
evasive
evil

excellent
excited
exclusive
exuberant

F
fabulous
faded
faint
fair
faithful
famous
fancy
fantastic
far-reaching
fascinated
fascinating
fashionable
fast
fat

fearless
few
fierce
filthy
fine
flaky
flashy
flat
flippant
fluffy
foolish
forgetful
frail

frank
frantic
freezing
French
fresh
friendly
frightened
frightening
full
functional
funny
furtive
fuzzy

G
generous
gentle
giant
gifted
gigantic
glamorous
glorious
golden

good
good-humored
gorgeous
gray
greasy
great
greedy

green
green-eyed
grieving
groundless
grubby
grumpy
guarded

H
hairy
hand-made
handsome
handwritten

happy
hard
hard-headed
harmful

harmless
harmonious
harsh
healthy

heavy
helpful
helpless
hesitant
high
hilarious
hissing

hollow
homeless
honorable
hopeless
horrible
hot
huge

hungry
hurt
hushed
husky
hyperactive
hypercritical

I

icy
ignorant
ill
illogical
imaginable
immense
immortal
impartial
impatient
impersonal

important
incredible
Indian
industrious
inexpensive
influential
insistent
instinctive
instructive

interested
interesting
intuitive
inventive
Irish
irregular
irresponsible
Italian
itchy

J K L

Japanese
jealous
jittery
jolly
joyous
juicy
justifiable
kind
kind-hearted
kindly

Korean
large
ladylike
late
lazy
Lebanese
lengthy
light
likeable
little

lively
lonely
long
long-lasting
loose
loud
lovely
loving
low
lucky

M N

magnificent
malicious
man-made

many
massive
materialistic

mathematical
mature
mean

melodic
melted
mighty
miniature
moaning
modern
mountainous
motherly
mouth-watering
much
mushy

musical
mute
mysterious
naïve
narrow
narrow-minded
nasty
national
naughty
near

nervous
never-ending
new
nice
no
nosy
noisy
numerous
nutritious
nutty

O P

obedient
odd
offensive
oily
old
old-fashioned
oldish
one
open
open-minded
orange
ordinary
out-of-date
outrageous
overdressed

painful
pale
pathetic
peaceful
perfect
perilous
persistent
personal
photographic
pink
placid
plain
plastic
plausible
pleasant

pleasurable
poetic
poisonous
possessive
powerful
precious
pretty
productive
progressive
protective
proud
punctual
puny
pure
purple

Q R

quadrennial
quaint
quarrelsome
queer
questionable
quick

quiet
rainy
rapid
rare
raspy
readable

ready
real
receptive
red
red-roofed
reflective

relieved
repulsive
resistible
resonant
responsible
restless

rich
righteous
ripe
roasted
robust
romantic

rotten
rough
round
Russian
rustic

S

sad
salty
sandy
scary
scattered
scrawny
secretive
selective
selfish
sensitive
shaggy
shaky
shallow
sharp
shivering
shocked
short
shy
sick
silent
silky
silly
simple
sincere

skilful
skinny
sleeveless
slimy
slippery
slow
small
smelly
smiling
smoky
smooth
sneaky
snobbish
soft
solid
some
sore
sour
sparkling
sparse
spicy
splendid
spotty

square
stale
steady
steep
sticky
stimulating
straight
strange
striped
strong
subconscious
submissive
subnormal
substantial
successful
sufficient
sun-dried
sulky
sunny
supernatural
sweet
swift
symbolic

T

talented
tall

tallish
tame

tameless
tan

tart
tasteless
tasty
tender
tense
terrible
terrific
testy
thankful

thick
thirsty
thoughtful
thoughtless
threatening
tight
time-consuming
timid
tiny

tired
tiresome
tough
tricky
troubled
true
truculent
two-legged
typical

U V

ugliest
ugly
unable
unbearable
uncapable
uncomfortable
undesirable
uneven
unexpected
unfair
unforgettable
unhappy

unilateral
uninterested
unkind
unsafe
unsightly
unsuitable
unsure
unusual
upset
uptight
vague

valuable
vast
venomous
victorious
vigorous
virtuous
vivacious
voiceless
volatile
voracious
vulgar

W Y Z

walled
warm
wary
washable
wasteful
waterproof
watery
weak
wealthy
weary
weekly

well-behaved
well-known
wet
white
wicked
wide
willing
windy
wise
witty
womanish

wonderful
wooded
wooden
world-famous
worried
worthless
wretched
wrong
yellow
yellowish
yielding

young	*youthful*	*zealous*
youngish	*zany*	*zippy*

MOST COMMON ADVERBS *(manner, place, time, frequency, degree)*[2]

MANNER

accidentally	*elegantly*	*hurriedly*
angrily	*enormously*	*inevitably*
anxiously	*enthusiastically*	*innocently*
awkwardly	*equally*	*irritably*
badly	*eventually*	*jointly*
beautifully	*exactly*	*joyously*
blindly	*faithfully*	*justly*
boldly	***fast***	*kindly*
bravely	*fatally*	*lazily*
brightly	*fiercely*	*loosely*
busily	*fondly*	*loudly*
calmly	*foolishly*	*madly*
carefully	*fortunately*	*mortally*
carelessly	*frankly*	*mysteriously*
cautiously	*frantically*	*neatly*
cheerfully	***friendly***	*nervously*
clearly	*generously*	*noisily*
closely	*gently*	*obediently*
correctly	*gladly*	*openly*
courageously	*gracefully*	*painfully*
cruelly	*greedily*	*patiently*
daringly	*happily*	*perfectly*
deliberately	***hard***	*politely*
doubtfully	*hastily*	*poorly*
eagerly	*healthily*	*powerfully*
early	*honestly*	*promptly*
easily	*hungrily*	*punctually*

2. Em negrito: advérbios com forma idêntica a adjetivos.

quickly
quietly
rapidly
rarely
really
recklessly
regularly
reluctantly
repeatedly
rightfully
roughly
rudely
sadly
safely
selfishly
sensibly
seriously

sharply
shyly
silently
sleepily
slowly
smoothly
softly
solemnly
speedily
stealthily
straight
stupidly
successfully
suddenly
suspiciously
swiftly

tenderly
tensely
thoughtfully
tightly
truthfully
unexpectedly
victoriously
violently
vivaciously
warmly
weakly
wearily
well
wildly
wisely
wrongly

PLACE

about
above
abroad
anywhere
away
back
backward/s
behind
below
down
downstairs
east

elsewhere
everywhere
far
here
in
indoors
inside
near
nearby
nowhere
off
on

out
outside
over
there
towards
under
underground
up
upstairs
upwards
where

TIME / FREQUENCY

after
again
ago

almost
already
always

annually
around
before

by
constantly
daily
during
early
eventually
ever
finally
first
for
formerly
frequently
generally
hardly
hourly
just

last
late
lately
never
next
no sooner
now
nowadays
occasionally
often
previously
quarterly
rarely
recently
regularly
seldom

shortly
since
sometimes
soon
still
then
thereafter
today
tomorrow
tonight
usually
weekly
yearly
yesterday
yet

DEGREE

absolutely
almost
awfully
badly
barely
completely
decidedly
deeply
enormously
enough
entirely
extremely
fairly
fully
greatly

hardly
highly
incredibly
indeed
intensely
just
least
less
little
most
much
nearly
practically
pretty

quite
rather
really
scarcely
simply
so
somewhat
strongly
terribly
thoroughly
too
totally
very
well

ADJECTIVES & PREPOSITIONS

Alguns adjetivos são acompanhados por determinadas preposições.
Os adjetivos destacados por (*) permitem mais de uma possibilidade.

OF

afraid	frightened	sick
ashamed	full	short
aware	guilty	stupid
capable	jealous	sure
certain	kind	suspicious
confident	nice	terrified
critical	proud	tired
envious	scared	typical
fond		

WITH

angry*	disappointed*	impressed*
annoyed	familiar	occupied
bored	friendly*	patient
busy	furious	pleased*
content	happy*	satisfied
crowded	honest	wrong
delighted		

TO

accustomed	inferior	polite
addicted	kind	possible
dedicated	married	rude
engaged	nice	superior
friendly*	opposed	similar
generous		

BY

amused	impressed*	surprised*
bored	shocked	

ABOUT

angry*	curious	pleased*
annoyed	depressed	right
anxious	disappointed*	sorry
careful	excited	upset
certain	happy*	worried
confused	nervous	

AT

amazed	excellent	skillful
angry*	good	surprised*
annoyed	lucky	useless
bad	skilled	

FOR

difficult	important	responsible
eager	late	sorry
famous	ready	suitable

FROM

absent	different	safe

IN

interested	involved

ON

keen	reliant

EXAMPLES

I am not afraid **of** spiders.
Is he angry **with** you?
She was very kind **to** me.
He is angry **about** my decision.
I'm good **at** English.

We were shocked **by** his speech.
That subject is difficult **for** me.
He is different **from** his father.
Are you interested **in** history?
They are keen **on** soccer.

Respostas
Answer Key

ADJECTIVES AND ADVERBS

ADJECTIVES

1. Underline the adjectives in the movie titles.

1. <u>Little Black</u> Swan
2. <u>Five Easy</u> Pieces
3. Creature from the <u>Black</u> Lagoon
4. The <u>Brown</u> Bunny
5. The <u>Talented</u> Mr. Ripley
6. <u>Unfortunate</u> Events
7. A <u>Better</u> World
8. A Book of <u>Common</u> Prayer
9. A <u>Brand New</u> Me
10. A <u>Cold</u> Case
11. A <u>Burning Hot</u> Summer
12. A Cat in Paris
13. A <u>Dirty</u> Job
14. A <u>Dark</u> Truth
15. The <u>Sixth</u> Man
16. <u>12 Angry</u> Men
17. <u>American</u> Beauty
18. <u>American</u> History X
19. At <u>First</u> Sight
20. A <u>Beautiful</u> Mind
21. <u>Deep</u> Impact
22. Defending <u>Your</u> Life
23. <u>Super</u> Mario Bros
24. Demetrius and the Gladiators
25. The Fellowship of the Ring
26. A <u>Few Good</u> Men
27. Fiddler on the Roof
28. Field of Dreams
29. The <u>Fifth</u> Element
30. Indiana Jones and the <u>Last</u> Crusade.

2. Choose the correct adjective.

1. *a*
2. *a*
3. *a*
4. *b*
5. *a*
6. *b*
7. *b*
8. *b*
9. *a*
10. *a*
11. *b*
12. *a*

3. Use adjectives from the box to expand the sentences.

1. *mysterious*
2. *thick*
3. *depressed*
4. *orange*
5. *heavy*
6. *good*
7. *Many/big*
8. *dusty*
9. *mountainous*
10. *star-shaped*
11. *white*
12. *calm*

4. Read the quotes. Classify the underlined words as **A** (adjective) or **N** (noun).

1. *N, A*
2. *A, A*
3. *A, N*
4. *N, N*
5. *A, A*
6. *A, A*
7. *A, N*
8. *N, N*
9. *A, N*
10. *A, A*

5. Check the sentences containing postpositive adjectives.

1. *available*
2. *useful*
5. *well-done*
6. *present*
7. *possible*
9. *imaginable*
10. *rich*

DEMONSTRATIVE, DISTRIBUTIVE AND POSSESSIVE ADJECTIVES

1. Classify the underlined words as **A** (adjective) or **P** (pronoun).
(A) 1, 2, 3, 5, 6, 7, 8, 10
(P) 4, 9

2. Check the correct demonstratives and correct the wrong ones.
Correct: 2, 3, 4, 6, 9
Incorrect: 1. That; 5. this; 7. those; 8. those; 10. this

3. Underline only the demonstrative adjectives and translate the sentences.

1. (such) *Eu nunca tinha visto tal livro.*
2. (that) *Este é um bom carro, mas prefiro aquele velho calhambeque.*
3. (these) *Ele comprou estas meias novas e doou aquelas para o time.*
4. (former) *Gostei mais do cantor anterior.*

5. *(such) Era uma história tão estúpida.*
6. *(xx) Esta tem sido uma década difícil para a Presidência dos Estados Unidos.*
7. *(such) Não tínhamos pago tais taxas antes.*
8. *(this) Ele se sentou neste lugar.*
9. *(those) Embora eu preferisse aquelas camisas, comprei estas.*
10. *(such) Acho tais pessoas muito aborrecidas.*

4. Choose the correct alternative.

1. *is*	6. *deserves*	11. *sees*
2. *suits*	7. *Either*	12. *soldier*
3. *each*	8. *has*	13. *is*
4. *every*	9. *day*	14. *each*
5. *boy*	10. *has*	15. *neither*

5. Classify the possessives as **A** (adjective) or **P** (pronoun).
Adjective: 1, 2, 3, 5, 7, 8, 10.
Pronoun: 4, 6, 9

6. Choose the correct adjective.

1. *Her*	6. *their*	11. *your*
2. *Their*	7. *her*	12. *my, her*
3. *Our*	8. *his*	13. *its*
4. *their*	9. *her*	14. *his*
5. *my*	10. *his*	15. *his*

INTERROGATIVE, QUANTITATIVE AND DESCRIPTIVE ADJECTIVES

1. Rewrite the sentences. Use *which*.
1. *Which language do you speak most fluently: Spanish, German, or Italian?*
2. *Which soccer team is the best: X, Y or W?*
3. *Which color is your book, red or white?*
4. *Which direction do I go: right or left/north or south?*
5. *Which color do you like best: blue, red or black?*

2. Complete the sentences.

1.	What	6.	What	11.	What
2.	Whose	7.	What	12.	What
3.	Which	8.	Which	13.	What
4.	Whose	9.	Which	14.	Which
5.	What	10.	Which	15.	What

3. Underline all quantitative adjectives.

1.	two	6.	little	11.	substantial
2.	many	7.	full	12.	Many
3.	few	8.	sufficient	13.	numerous
4.	Several	9.	enough	14.	enough
5.	all	10.	any	15.	Some

4. Underline the correct alternative.

1.	much	5.	enough	8.	little
2.	any	6.	no	9.	no
3.	whole	7.	little	10.	all
4.	some				

5. Choose the correct alternatives to complete the text.

1.	fresh	3.	terrible	5.	heavy
2.	dirty	4.	hot	6.	little

6. Complete the sentences with adjectives from the box.

1.	first	3.	first/Brazilian	5.	famous
2.	expensive	4.	largest		

7. Rewrite the adjective in parentheses in the correct place.
1. No <u>two</u> zebras have the same stripes.
2. The giraffe has no <u>vocal</u> cords.
3. Goat's eyes have <u>rectangular</u> pupils.
4. A zebra is white with <u>black</u> stripes.
5. Happy, a female <u>Asian</u> elephant recognized herself in the mirror.
6. George Washington's <u>favorite</u> horse was named Lexington.
7. Ancient Egyptians believed that cats were <u>sacred</u> animals.

8. *The ostrich's vigorous legs are <u>powerful</u> enough to kill a man.*
9. *All polar bears are <u>left-handed</u>.*
10. *A cat's urine glows under a <u>black</u> light.*
11. *Grizzly bears have long claws about the length of a <u>human</u> finger.*
12. *Cats cannot survive on a <u>vegetarian</u> diet.*
13. *Camels have three eyelids to protect themselves from <u>blowing</u> sand.*
14. *Chameleons can move their eyes in two <u>different</u> directions at the same time*
15. *<u>Brown</u> eggs come from hens with red feathers and red ear lobes.*

ORDER OF ADJECTIVES

1. Match the sentence parts.

A		B		C	
1.	*b*	*6.*	*e*	*11.*	*e*
2.	*c*	*7.*	*a*	*12.*	*b*
3.	*d*	*8.*	*d*	*13.*	*a*
4.	*a*	*9.*	*c*	*14.*	*d*
5.	*e*	*10.*	*b*	*15.*	*c*

2. Check the correct adjective order.

1.	*three empty*	*9.*	*big, old, black*
2.	*a pretty, old*	*10.*	*old, white, brick*
3.	*an international singing*	*11.*	*a wonderful old Italian*
4.	*an interesting, old*	*12.*	*large, prehistoric*
5.	*an expensive big*	*13.*	*big square blue*
6.	*fresh British*	*14.*	*black, Italian*
7.	*a big, dark-haired*	*15.*	*three little*
8.	*fine, old*		

3. Write **C** (for correct) or **I** (for incorrect sentences).
Correct: 1, 3, 4, 5, 6, 10, 11, 14, 15
Incorrect: 2, 7, 8, 9, 12, 13

2. *Centuries ago books were made of wood and were heavy.*

7. *Dolphins are extremely social beings and have "sophisticated" language.*
8. *Elisha Otis invented the brake used in modern elevators.*
9. *She's a very calm person.*
12. *Ancient Japanese thought that earthquakes were caused by a giant spider living under the earth.*
13. *Howler monkeys are the noisiest land animals.*

4. Read the sentences about London. Write **C** (for correct) and **I** (for incorrect sentences).
Correct: 1, 2, 3, 6
Incorrect: 4, 5

FORM OF ADJECTIVES

1. Add *-ful* and *-less* to create adjectives. Translate the new words.
1. *careful (cuidadoso), careless (descuidado)*
2. *colorful (colorido), colorless (sem cor)*
3. *doubtful (duvidoso), doubtless (indubitável)*
4. *faithful (fiel), faithless (infiel)*
5. *forceful (coercitivo), forceless (sem força)*
6. *fruitful (frutífero), fruitless (infrutífero)*
7. *powerful (potente), powerless (impotente)*
8. *tasteful (saboroso), tasteless (sem gosto)*

2. Add *–able* to create adjectives. Translate the new words.
1. *acceptable (aceitável)*
2. *bearable (suportável)*
3. *believable (acreditável)*
4. *comparable (comparável)*
5. *desirable (desejável)*
6. *drinkable (potável)*
7. *predictable (previsível)*
8. *washable (lavável)*

3. Add *-ive* to create adjectives. Translate the new words.
1. *attractive (atrativo)*
2. *constructive (construtivo)*
3. *expansive (expansivo)*
4. *expensive (caro)*
5. *explosive (explosivo)*
6. *instructive (instrutivo)*
7. *offensive (ofensivo)*
8. *talkative (falante)*

4. Add the correct suffix to create new adjectives.

accidental, dangerous, long, starry, windy
comical, corrective, reddish, elderly

5. Choose the correct participles to complete the sentences.

1.	*frightened*	*3.*	*bored*	*5.*	*fascinated*
2.	*exhausting*	*4.*	*depressing*	*6.*	*exciting*

6. Complete the sentences with the correct adjectives.

1.	*well-behaved*	*4.*	*long-lasting*	*6.*	*cold-blooded*
2.	*a red-eyed*	*5.*	*old-fashioned*	*7.*	*low-cost*
3.	*brightly-lit*				

7. Rewrite the expressions. Follow the example.

1.	*a six-year-old cat*	*5.*	*a black-haired man*
2.	*a life-changing adventure*	*6.*	*a six-month-old baby*
3.	*a decision-making process*	*7.*	*a part-time worker*
4.	*a narrow-minded man*		

8. Write the correct adjective. Follow the example.

1.	*race horse*	*14.*	*article writer*
2.	*horse race*	*15.*	*Sunday picnic*
3.	*love story*	*16.*	*wedding dress*
4.	*billiards table*	*17.*	*news editor*
5.	*boat race*	*18.*	*dog food*
6.	*computer exhibition*	*19.*	*delicious dog food*
7.	*clothes shop*	*20.*	*car salesman*
8.	*tennis shoes*	*21.*	*honest car salesman*
9.	*golf balls*	*22.*	*football team coach*
10.	*athletics trainers*	*23.*	*coffee jar*
11.	*sports clubs*	*24.*	*empty coffee jar*
12.	*accounts department*	*25.*	*convention centre*
13.	*English teacher*		

ADVERBS

1. Answer the questions. Use the adverbs in parentheses.
1. *He drives fast.*
2. *She went to school.*
3. *I was born in June.*
4. *She drinks coffee every morning.*
5. *He speaks English badly.*

2. Classify the underlined adverbs as **M** (manner), **P** (place), **T** (time), **F** (frequency) or **D** (degree).

1. *F*	6. *T*	11. *P*
2. *M*	7. *F*	12. *M*
3. *T*	8. *D*	13. *T*
4. *P*	9. *T*	14. *P*
5. *F*	10. *M*	15. *D*

3. Choose the correct adverb.

1. *badly*	6. *well*	11. *really*
2. *easily*	7. *never*	12. *rarely*
3. *softly*	8. *perfectly*	13. *once*
4. *evidently*	9. *carefully*	14. *upstairs*
5. *easily*	10. *often*	15. *straight*

4. Underline the adverbs.

1. *abroad*	6. *incredibly / slowly*	11. *angrily*
2. *really*	7. *Honestly*	12. *usually / very*
3. *extremely / fast*	8. *often*	13. *fast*
4. *extremely*	9. *late*	14. *quietly*
5. *Obviously*	10. *only*	15. *happily*

5. Choose the correct relative adverb.

1. *where*	5. *when*	8. *where*
2. *when*	6. *when*	9. *why*
3. *why*	7. *where*	10. *where*
4. *where*		

6. Complete with the correct alternative.

1.	*wrongly*	*5.*	*properly*	*8.*	*easily*
2.	*approximately*	*6.*	*always*	*9.*	*highly*
3.	*frequently*	*7.*	*well*	*10.*	*yearly*
4.	*nearly*				

POSITION AND ORDER OF ADVERBS

1. Write the adverbs of manner in the correct sentences.

1.	*dangerously*	*3.*	*fast*	*5.*	*quietly*
2.	*nicely*	*4.*	*well*	*6.*	*easily*

2. Write the adverbs of place in the correct sentences.

1.	*outside*	*3.*	*somewhere*	*5.*	*nearby*
2.	*downstairs*	*4.*	*upstairs*	*6.*	*there*

3. Write the adverbs of time in the correct sentences.

1.	*next*	*3.*	*during*	*5.*	*already*
2.	*for*	*4.*	*lately*	*6.*	*yesterday*

4. Place the adverbs with the verbs.

1. *We sometimes go...*
2. *It is always hot...*
3. *It never snows...*
4. *I seldom meet my...*
5. *Grandma usually sleeps...*
6. *I have often been to...*

5. Rewrite the sentences and place the adverbs correctly.

1. *The man drove really badly.*
2. *The dentist is upstairs.*
3. *I seldom walk my dog.*
4. *The water was extremely cold.*
5. *My sister is very beautiful.*
6. *Grandma can hear well.*

7. *I have never seen you.*
8. *They immensely enjoyed the play./They enjoyed the play immensely.*
9. *We entirely agree with you./We agree with you entirely.*
10. *Last month we were in London./We were in London last month.*

6. Check all possible positions for the words in parentheses.
1. ☑ *She waited ☑.*
2. *We ☐ don't swim ☑.*
3. *☐ They are ☑ exhausted from the trip ☐.*
4. *My brother ☑ plays ☐ the flute in the morning.*
5. *He ☐ walked ☑.*
6. *You are ☑ young to drive ☐.*
7. *I saw ☐ you ☑.*
8. *He drove ☑ dangerously ☐.*
9. *She ☐ was ☑ sad.*
10. *I speak ☐ English ☑.*

7. Rewrite the sentences and place the words in parentheses in the correct position.
1. *in Jamaica last week*   4. *there in a hurry*
2. *very windy this morning*   5. *very carefully*
3. *very hard yesterday*

8. Find out the wrong alternative.
1. *b*   3. *b*   5. *c*
2. *a*   4. *b*

FORM OF ADVERBS

1. Transform the adjectives into adverbs.
1. *gently*   6. *angrily*   11. *probably*
2. *fairly*   7. *terribly*   12. *possibly*
3. *loudly*   8. *boringly*   13. *richly*
4. *happily*   9. *luckily*   14. *safely*
5. *basically*   10. *carefully*

2. Underline the adverbs.

1. seriously
2. really
3. truly
4. slowly
5. angrily
6. happily
7. carelessly
8. fluently
9. happily
10. annually

3. Complete the sentence using adverbs.

1. quickly
2. beautifully
3. relatively
4. nicely
5. dramatically
6. easily
7. happily
8. slowly
9. poorly
10. carefully

4. Choose the correct word.

1. b. shortly
2. a. truly
3. b. well
4. a. extremely
5. b. badly
6. a. carelessly
7. a. bitterly
8. b. frequently
9. a. seriously
10. a. easily
11. b. loudly
12. b. daily
13. a. monthly
14. b. suspiciously
15. a. courageously

5. Complete the sentences with words from the box.

1. nearly
2. really
3. hardly
4. early
5. shortly
6. lately
7. late
8. well
9. badly
10. deeply

6. Write down the correct adverb to complete the chart.

1. reliably
2. economically
3. helpfully
4. attentively
5. disappointingly
6. charmingly
7. breathlessly
8. tiredly

7. Match the synonyms.

1. a
2. c
3. e
4. d
5. b
6. f

ADJECTIVE OR ADVERB?

1. Underline the adjectives.

1. *heavy*
2. *clear*
3. *black*
4. *positive*
5. *fantastic*
6. *general, great*
7. *grizzly, large, different, black*
8. *small, African*
9. *accidental*
10. *calmest*

2. Underline the adverbs.

1. *never*
2. *exceedingly, far*
3. *daily*
4. *fast*
5. *always*
6. *seldom*
7. *incredibly, quickly*
8. *very*
9. *amazingly, high*
10. *extremely, confidently*

3. Classify the underlined words as **Adj.** (adjective) or **Adv.** (adverb).
Adj.: 1, 3, 6, 7, 10, 12, 14
Adv.: 2, 4, 5, 8, 9, 11, 13, 15

4. Choose the correct alternative to complete the sentence.

1. *timid, softly*
2. *harder*
3. *possibly*
4. *quadrennially*
5. *slowly*
6. *tired*
7. *extremely*
8. *modern*
9. *well*
10. *surprisingly*
11. *completely*
12. *certainly*
13. *dark*
14. *quickly*
15. *Unfortunately*

5. Complete the sentences with words from the box.

1. *sadly*
2. *nicely*
3. *heavily*
4. *lazily*
5. *truly*
6. *wholly*
7. *simply*
8. *tragically*
9. *furiously*
10. *quickly*

COMPARISON OF ADJECTIVES AND ADVERBS

1. Write the comparative and superlative forms of these adjectives.

1. *thinner, thinnest*
2. *bigger, biggest*
3. *better, best*
4. *older, oldest*
5. *more expensive, most expensive*
6. *shorter, shortest*
7. *later, latest*
8. *heavier, heaviest*
9. *more interesting, most interesting*
10. *worse, worst*

2. Write the comparative and superlative forms of these adverbs.
1. *nearer, nearest*
2. *more proudly, most proudly*
3. *more quickly, most quickly*
4. *more dangerously, most dangerously*
5. *better, best*
6. *worse, worst*
7. *more heavily, most heavily*
8. *more sadly, most sadly*
9. *more slowly, most slowly*
10. *faster, fastest*

3. Complete the sentences with the comparative form of the words in parentheses.

1. *better*	6. *more*	11. *smaller/more agile*
2. *longer*	7. *smarter*	12. *more*
3. *bigger*	8. *more*	13. *more attractive*
4. *weaker*	9. *faster*	14. *less*
5. *faster*	10. *larger*	15. *more aggressive*

4. Complete the sentences with the superlative form of the words in parentheses.

1. *laziest*	4. *most common*	7. *brainiest*
2. *most intelligent*	5. *fastest*	8. *fastest*
3. *best*	6. *smartest/cleanest*	9. *largest*

10. loudest	**12.** deepest	**14.** shortest/longest
11. most acute	**13.** longest	**15.** largest/smallest

5. Circle the correct alternative.

1. a	**5.** a	**9.** a
2. b	**6.** a	**10.** b
3. b	**7.** b	**11.** b
4. b	**8.** a	**12.** b

6. Complete the sentences with the expressions from the box.

1. the better	**3.** the cheaper	**5.** the sooner
2. the higher	**4.** the more difficult	**6.** the less

7. Match the sentence parts.

1. a	**3.** b	**5.** c
2. f	**4.** e	**6.** d

8. Choose the correct word to complete the expressions.

1. busy	**6.** white	**11.** clear
2. old	**7.** red	**12.** easy
3. flat	**8.** big	**13.** free
4. soon	**9.** cold	**14.** sick
5. quiet	**10.** hungry	**15.** innocent

COMMON MISTAKES

1. Check the sentence containing only as adjective.
Adjectives: 3, 5

2. Match sentence to meaning.

1. b	**3.** d
2. c	**4.** a

3. Complete the sentences using enough. Then check **Adj.** (for adjective) or **Adv.** (for adverb).

1. *enough chairs (adj.)*
2. *old enough (adv.)*
3. *slowly enough (adv.)*
4. *hard enough (adv.)*
5. *enough support (adj.)*
6. *hot enough (adv.)*
7. *enough sandwiches (adj.)*

4. Underline the correct alternative.

1. *slowly*
2. *well*
3. *good*
4. *too*
5. *bad; badly*
6. *sure*
7. *too*
8. *good*
9. *shortly*
10. *well*
11. *good*
12. *well*
13. *very*
14. *nearly*
15. *short*

5. Complete the sentences. Use *fairly* or *rather*.

1. *fairly*
2. *rather*
3. *fairly*
4. *rather*
5. *rather*
6. *fairly*
7. *rather*
8. *rather*
9. *rather*
10. *fairly*

6. Complete the sentences. Use yet, *still* or *already*.

1. *already/yet*
2. *still*
3. *yet*
4. *still, already*
5. *already*
6. *already*
7. *still*
8. *already*
9. *yet*
10. *still*

7. Rewrite the sentences. Use inversion.

1. *Never had she done that before.*
2. *Seldom is Joseph late.*
3. *Nowhere could the dog be found.*
4. *Almost had I finished the chapter when he arrived.*
5. *Under no circumstances can I accept cheques.*
6. *On the doorstep was a bunch of flowers.*
7. *Never have I felt so calm.*

Este livro foi composto nas fontes Stag e Mercury e impresso em outubro de 2013
pela gráfica Vida e Consciência, sobre papel offset $90g/m^2$.